CONVERSATIONS WITH THE KAGAWONG RIVER

CONVERSATIONS WITH
THE KAGAWONG RIVER

POEMS

SOPHIE ANNE EDWARDS

TALONBOOKS

Talonbooks
9259 Shaughnessy Street, Vancouver, British Columbia, Canada V6P 6R4
talonbooks.com

Talonbooks is located on xʷməθkʷəy̓əm, Sḵwx̱wú7mesh, and səlilwətaɫ Lands.

First printing: 2024

Typeset in Calibri and EB Garamond
Printed and bound in Canada on 100% post-consumer recycled paper

Cover photograph by sophie anne edwards

Talonbooks acknowledges the financial support of the Canada Council for the Arts, the Government of Canada through the Canada Book Fund, and the Province of British Columbia through the British Columbia Arts Council and the Book Publishing Tax Credit.

Library and Archives Canada Cataloguing in Publication

Title: Conversations with the Kagawong River : poems / sophie anne edwards.
Names: edwards, sophie anne, author.
Description: Includes some text in Anishinaabemowin.
Identifiers: Canadiana 2024042252X | ISBN 9781772016246 (softcover)
Subjects: LCGFT: Poetry.
Classification: LCC PS8609.D87 C66 2024 | DDC C811/.6—dc23

For Martin, biologist and artist
1967–2004
Finally, here's the book you asked me to write.

Statement from Alan Ojiig Corbiere

As a settler and ally, sophie has written a creative and meaningful book that, from the "other side," grapples with a decolonial approach to writing about, and with, place – a place significant to both the Anishinaabeg of Mnidoo Mnising and settlers. The book, in its inclusion of Anishinaabe-mowin River terms, our translations of historical plaques, and its building of a broader ecocultural and geographical story of the Gaagigewang Ziibi, contributes to uncovering an important local toponym and revealing historical truths. I have known sophie for many years and worked with her on a couple of projects; we've had many conversations about our academic projects and about local history and traditional knowledge over tea. She's worked steadily to build local awareness about our history and the impacts of colonization and to build people's connection to local ecosystems. I'm glad to see her finding ways to integrate historical truths and challenging dominant relations through a creative approach, which will reach a broad audience and bring more visibility and accessibility to our efforts at language revitalization and historical truth-telling. Sometimes creativity and art reach places where words – particularly English ones – can't.

—Dr. Alan Ojiig Corbiere
Historian and language advocate
M'Chigeeng First Nation and York University

Statement from Art Jacko

It is my pleasure to extend support for sophie's book *Conversations with the Kagawong River*. It is good to see that sophie has continued to support efforts to build awareness of local Anishinaabeg and treaty history.

The inclusion of the Anishinaabemowin translations of Kagawong's historical plaques, which were originally created by a language team from M'Chigeeng First Nation, led by Dr. Alan Corbiere, is good to see. These, along with additional Anishinaabemowin River terms, support our community's efforts at language revitalization. The book expands on the history included in the Kagawong plaques by documenting the Indigenous cemetery, gardens, and paths, contributing to a more fulsome accounting of these sites and Anishinaabeg history.

—Art Jacko
  Enaagdenjged (CAO / Band Manager)
  M'Chigeeng First Nation

Statement from Josh Eshkawkogan

In our journey of life it's very important that we acknowledge each other, so I am acknowledging you, and your gifts. You have a lot of knowledge about Indigenous ways that was passed on to you by all the people that you've met and worked with in this Traditional Territory of Manitoulin, through teachings, work with the land, the ceremonies that you've attended. You're very capable of understanding the natural law of our Territory. So that's why I support you to keep going, and to keep doing what you're doing in regards to sharing your wisdom, giving your perspective of the land you're working on, the stories you're working on, the people you're working with.

When you create something such as a book, or whatever we do, it's all about creation in regards to what the Creator gave you. The Creator gave you that gift of putting words together to understand who we are, so I'm happy to be able to say that I acknowledge you for the gift of writing that you do about Indigenous ways and understanding Indigenous knowledge of where we are, like Gaagigewang, "where the mist comes up."

All these things that our young people don't understand – you're bringing something "out front" for people to see in regards to what these special places mean to us as Indigenous people. But not just Indigenous people. Like the Bridal Veil Falls, that's a big attraction for people from around the world. Being able to have someone like you to represent and to admire the beauty of Kagawong is a gift you've provided, so I appreciate you.

You're very capable of understanding the language for what it means to us as Indigenous people, and understanding the elements of life that we have, and you're honouring them. That's what you do, you provide those elements to us through your work. Sometimes we need to awaken ourselves to those things, and that's what you do.

Some people may say you're using white person's privilege, but in today's society, there's a lot of people that need to carry the language whether they're Indigenous or not. We're put on this land base in order to help people, however that is, so if it's the Indigenous way, that is the way it is, whether they're Indigenous or not. It's about acceptance of one another, and what each person's gifts are, and each other's bundles. It's not the colour of your tongue, it's about who you are in spirit.

It's very important that people understand the writer, especially if you're reading her book. You want to know exactly where she's coming from. I've known you for a long time, since I worked at Kenjgewin Teg and you came in to work with us. That's how we connected to each other, working with the Land, experiencing what the Land means to us. Your daughter was learning at Kenjgewin Teg too. We became real good friends. We did ceremonies together. These are quality friendships that we accumulate and we never let them go. My friendship with you means a lot to me. So I honour your gift of putting words together, how you put your words in place, I honour the wisdom that you've gathered. To put your book in place and your words in place, that's a gift.

—Ojibwe Elder Josh Eshkawkogan
   Wiikwemkoong First Nation
   Elder in residence at the Noojmowin Teg Health Centre

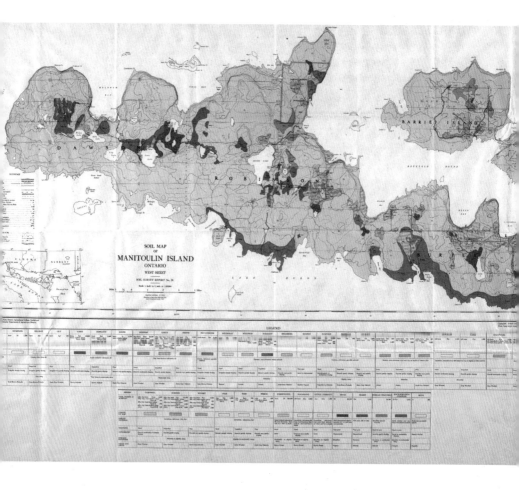

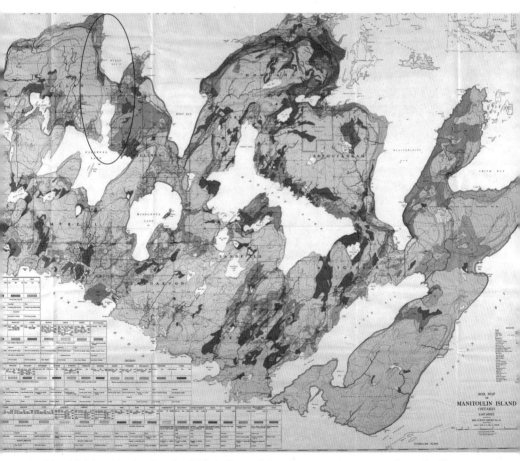

Mnidoo Mnising, Manitoulin Island. The village of Gaagigewang, Kagawong, where the River runs from Lake Kagawong into Mudge Bay.

Gaagigewang Ziibi, Kagawong River

Kinoonaan Ziibin, Conversations with the River

Ziibi: River.

Ziibiiyaajmowin: River story.

Kagawong: A small village on Manitoulin Island, Mnidoo Mnising in northeastern Ontario, territory of the Anishinaabeg (Ojibwe, Odawa, and Potawatomi). The Island – apart from the Wiikwemkoong First Nation Unceded – currently falls within the 1862 Manitoulin Island Treaty / Treaty 94.

Bridal Veil Falls: This area of Kagawong was known by Anishinaabeg residents as Gaagigewang (Kagawong), which translates as "always foggy" or "where falling water throws a mist." | Niibwi-Aagwiingwebzowin nbiish bngising (gakaabikaang) giiwta'iinh gii-zhi-gkendaagwod gonda Anishinaabeg gaa-bi-dnokiijig Gaagigewang, mii dash wi edming aabjiwang (pane awang) maage awanbiisaamgad nbiish bi-nji-bngising.

Ecology: From the Greek οἶκος, oikos, meaning "household," "home," or "dwelling." For an Anishinaabemowin translation, Alan Corbiere suggests endaayaan, "where I live/reside"; and adds, "out west I have seen wenji-bimaadiziyaang, 'from where I derive my livelihood/sustenance,' so perhaps 'enji-bmaadziyaang.'"

Zaagaa Aki ("love the land"), **Mooshkaa Shikmaa Kwe** ("feel Mother Earth, the land loves us and helps us heal"): While there isn't a specific word for resilience in Anishinaabemowin, Ojibwe elder Josh Eshkawkogan (Wiikwemkoong Unceded) says "resilience" can be roughly translated as "how strong is your heart, how strong is your connection to the land."

Kinoonaan ziibi: Sounding with or conversing with a River; literal translation, "s/he is speaking to the River": a process through which the writer grapples with loving an occupied landscape and the necessity for a wholly other set of relations. Learning to listen.

Ndoo-nsastaan ziibi: "Ndoo-nsastaan is a powerful word to mean I understand how things are alive, I understand the laws of nature, I am in relationship, I understand what's happening at the River," Josh Eshkawkogan.

Megwenyig: Stranger.

Megwenh ndaaw, e-megtawgwazid: A stranger who speaks a strange language.

Zhaagnaash (m), zhaagnaashiikwe (f): Offshore person, someone who has come across the water; this is the common usage for settler. Local elders and first speakers also use eshkibgamshkaad, one newly arrived to this land.

Settler and Settler Colonialism: A settler is a person who occupies socio-political and cultural space and land, directly and indirectly and in concert with the legacy of (neo)colonization and its injustices (settler colonialism). Not an event in the past: an ongoing project and process.

Conversations With My Toes Dipping into the Water at the Bend Along the Lower River Where the Water Pools Before Rushing Around the Bend and Over the Clay Deposits

Over two years, I spend time on the Gaagigewang Ziibi, Kagawong River learning to listen to her.

be attentive   give an audience   to tune in   give attention
eavesdrop   hang on words   pick up on
overhear   take into consideration   mind
receive   concentrate   welcome

Evaporation from the River joins the water from Lake Huron
to become rain and snow, falling on me
an average of 744 mm per year.

Residence time: the average time that water spends in a particular location or cycle.

The River replenishes herself about every sixteen days
water from Mud Creek flows into Lake Kagawong into the River
then into Mudge Bay and Lake Huron
also into the water line that feeds my house.

To listen is to understand the River as a speaker.
The River races over the falls, hushes along the slows
murmurs in the shallows, rifles over the   rocks   and branches
burbles in the pools   races around the bends.

To listen as a geographer and a writer is to understand the River as an animate, lively subject; is also to consider the marks, traces, patterns, calls, sounds, movements as texts in languages that I don't speak, but might hear, feel, see. A site or a subject with a history, a story.

I want to hear the River, expand the definitions of subject, text, author, and listener. To attempt to listen on the River's terms.

conversation   chat
gabble   natter   parlay
visit talk   exchange
sound with

The biota, seasonal changes, and various processes of the River's systems become the primary text, the first language, and the first author.

Resist the presumption that texts
are only constructed and communicated by humans
and for humans, restricted to the printed word.
Open to the possibility that the River
has agency, a range of languages beyond what I hear, see, and apprehend,
even possibly the capacity to engage with my human texts, to read me.

Uncanny. Magical. Outside normal understanding.

The Gaagigewang Ziibi is far more than a text.

"*Geography*" from Greek "geo-," "gê," earth, and "-graphia," "gráphō," writing.

Extend human description
to collaborative writing
to the earth writing herself.
It may be true that the River
can't write or tell a story
but there's a great deal of beauty,
magic, and meaning that might come
from believing, and acting, like it is possible.
There is something important
about not knowing
something good about
being tentative.
Certain certainties, earthly calamity.

"Landscape" is a term that geographers grapple with, along with concepts of space and place. "Space" as a concept isn't down under the stones with the caddis fly larvae or on its knees looking at the gentle jack-in-the-pulpit. "Place" can easily erase ecologies and contestations. Land is where my body lives. Land is where colonization, climate change, and my body meet.

The land and her extensive, interdisciplinary, boundary-resisting network of family.

I want to sit with the River
try to hear what she might say
about herself
if she might teach me to listen
and to listen differently.

I am told, the land is animate
    active, an agent – the River as *she*.
        I enter into the rapids
        bang up against stones
my/settler histories
                    Anishinaabe world views
        that are not mine.
                    Limitations of my language.

    There is a biotic world that exists
beyond me
        is not available for me
                    to understand.
I wade in, anyway,
            knowing that learning a new language –
the many languages of the River,
        the creatures, plants, and trees
                that live together there –
                is an opening gesture, a greeting, a need for time

        a lifetime.

    the River is not out there
            she is also running through me.
    I wade into her
        I drink the River and the sediments
    running with her
        am observed, felt
a reversal of observation.
        I am "other than River"
                and also of the River,
    we write each other.

    I'm falling into ecology,
            falling into the River
        falling into creative unfolding
composing, de-compos*ing*
                the not knowing
        of what I'm doing, or not doing.
    The truly awkward aspect of it
            as a writer learning to write
                and a human learning to listen and
                        sound with a River.

First Treaty

Wa mshiikenh boonmad zhibiiganan meznaabkigaadegin siniin maamwi dbaad'daanaawaa aankeyaadziwin miinwaa go maamoonji-ntam waawiindmaagewin, wi Debenjged gaa-zhi-waawiindmawaad Anishinaaben (Odaawaag, Ojibweg, Boodewaadmiig). Mdaaswi-shi-nswi waawnoon naabshkaagemgadoon mdaaswi-shi-nswi giizoonsag wi mooshkin ngo-bboongag, miinwaa aabji aanji-waawiindmaadwaad Debeanjged miinwaa Anishinaabeg wi Mshiikenh-Mnis aabdeg pane da-ni-temgad waa-ni-aanji-bmaadziwaad.

The turtle/egg petroglyph speaks to replenishment, the life cycle, and also to the first Treaty – that between the Anishinaabeg (Odaawaa, Ojibwe, and Potawatomi) and the Creator. The thirteen eggs represent the thirteen moons of a full year's cycle, and the constant, repeating commitment (Treaty) between the Creator and the Anishinaabeg, that Turtle Island (North America) will always be there to replenish them.

Prophesy

As the prophecies
foretold, however, the bands [the Ojibwe,
Potawatomi, and Odawa] were reunited several
generations later at Manitoulin Island, forming a union
known as the Three Fires Confederacy that remains to this day. In
the time of the Third Fire, they found the place foretold in prophecy,
"where the food grows on the water," and established their new homelands
in the country of wild rice. The people lived well for a long time under the care of
maples and birches, sturgeon and beaver, eagle and loon. The spiritual teachings
that had guided them kept the people strong and together they flourished in the
bosom of their nonhuman relatives. At the time of the Fourth Fire, the history of
another people came to be braided into ours. Two prophets arose among the people,
foretelling the coming of the light-skinned people in ships from the east, but their
visions differed in what was to follow. The path was not clear, as it cannot be with
the future. The first prophet said that if the offshore people, the zaaganaash, came
in brotherhood, they would bring great knowledge. Combined with Anishinaabe
ways of knowing, this would form a great new nation. But the second prophet
sounded a warning: He said that what looks like the face of brotherhood might
be the face of death. These new people might come with brotherhood, or
they might come with greed for the riches of our land. How would we
know which face is the true one? If the fish became poisoned and
the water unfit to drink, we would know which face they
wore. And for their actions the zaaganaash came
to be known instead as chimokman — the
long-knife people.

—Robin Wall Kimmerer in *Braiding Sweetgrass*

Uncanny Sounds

zhaagnaashiikwe ndaaw I am a settler
megwenh ndaaw   e-megtawgwazid, a stranger who speaks
a language   translation   strange to this River
I speak the   mist adaptation   uncanny sounds
that do not   surface reading   have a history
connected to   transition decoding riparian   this place sounds
that are not   rephrasing surface tension   entwined with
the   transliteration evaporation   resonance of the Anishinaabeg
the world   metaphrase adsorption   seems both more defined
and less   rendering transformation   so seen
through the   liminality   surface of the River

I want to become   comfortable
with the strange mix   of familiarity   and estrangement

How to translate the spirit sound of the River   Gaagigewang Ziibi

These definitions of settler
do not capture the claiming
the displacement that the word "settler" does
but they do articulate the strangeness of my relations

My own otherness   the space between me
and the River between   eerie   me and the Anishinaabeg
cannot be   exceptional   broached through a language
that does not   magical devilish   speak River or speak with it
a language that   ghostly unearthly weird   does not understand
or carry a   unheard-of   relational world view
a language   unnatural   that carries the distance
that opens with   customary enchanted   the act of claiming
My language   earthly common   body   position
a complex mix   familiar usual   of resistances
and   natural   collaborations

Through the process of writing this book
which began as a desire to spend time on the River
I found I didn't have the language to write about
or with or from the River
and so I found myself instead
trying to work from the space
between me and the River.

Using the language in the context of a colonized territory, where languages have been stolen or forbidden, is fraught. Choosing to include Anishinaaabemowin words in this book is an effort to loosen the grip of my colonizing language, settler claims. I hope these inclusions act not as a claim, but as an incantation, a call to the River, to the language of its relations.

Uncanny

The water of my body
greets the water of the River. I open
my mouth and expel the last of the air in my
lungs, language flowing out of my mouth, the only
language that is sensible – that of my air, that of the water
of my body, that of air passing through my lungs and across
my tongue. I hear my heartbeat and feel the pulse of the River.
The shifting River is pleasing, a release from definition, from the
idea of self. Translation is a space of transition, like mist, like the
riparian, water becoming vapour, land becoming River. Momentarily
I understand, but the need for breath follows me below the surface.
Even submerged, I know I am other, an uncanny body with an uncanny
tongue. The River accepts my strangeness, filters it, swallows it, and
will swallow me completely. I would like to become uncanny in the
magical sense of the word. Be able to understand the language
of the River. Shift from the canniness of colonial heritage,
from being something hard to explain. Translation
is the space I can inhabit/borrow, where I can
breathe between two worlds, air and
water, English and ecosystem.

water

language

tongue

transition

filters

Translation

worlds

Instructions for the Poet Wanting to Sound with the Gaagigewang Ziibi

1. lose my language (attempt translation) shift the subject
   interview worms, trees. try to hold space in the space between languages
   unsettle my nouns, become verb

2. listen to what the River speaks about history, follow its breath
   do not dig in the earth, lay on the banks with the rot of leaves
   and dying salmon, leave no trace (desire is a trace)

3. map lines, traces, patterns. note the limitations of the visual
   close the naked eye, open my ears
   avoid settler stories and the stasis of archives (maps are power)

4. write through my feet, sink my fingers into borer traces and otter holes
   document what is natural and what isn't, switch categories, undo Nature
   (my body is historically contingent)

5. hope for collaboration, give up on the capacity to
   apprehend complexity. landscape is constructed
   my alphabet is constructed. open my mouth (silence)

6. stop reading, write less, abandon time and dead lines
   ponder my lost capacity to predict the weather
   (what we know is momentary, in slow time speeding up)

7. create poems that will go where everything will go when the earth
   can no longer sustain us. hope for more than taking, something
   beyond solace (edit for three-degree warming)

   this is where someone else should speak
   this is where the River should be
   (this is not my River)

Directive, 1861

the grant to
each Head of a family
of twenty-five acres as
his own property will more
than compensate them for
any imaginary interest
they may have in
the island.

*Directive to William Bartlett, the
superintendant of Indian Affairs for
the Central Superintendancy, from
Vankoughnet, the commissioner of
Crown Lands and superintendant
general of Indian Affairs, 1861.
The strategy was to rescind the
earlier 1836 Bond Head Treaty,
which provided the entire Island
to the Anishinaabeg.*

... the commissioners
learned that the Indians "were
indisposed to listen to terms for the
surrender of the island." Moreover, "for two
years past they have been expecting that some
proposition would be made to them for this purpose,
and during the last winter councils were held to
determine the question in advance," and the young men
had tried to persuade the chiefs "to refuse to listen to any
terms for a surrender of any portion of the island." Though
the objective of the commissioner's council had not yet
been announced, "the Indians had become possessed
of the idea, that it related to the settlement of the
Island by the white population, and they had
resolved almost unanimously to oppose
any proposal to that effect."

Treaty Clauses Four and Five, 1862

Treaty
clause Four. Fourthly:
Should any lot or lots, selected
as aforesaid, be contiguous to any bay or
harbour, or any stream of water upon which a mill
site shall be found, and should the Government be of
opinion that such lot or lots ought to be reserved for the
use of the public, or for village or park lots, or such mill site be
sold with a view to the erection of a mill thereon, and shall signify
such its opinion through its proper agent, then the Indian who
has selected, or who wishes to select such lot shall make another
selection, but if he has made any improvements thereon he shall
be allowed a fair compensation therefor. Fifthly: The selections
shall all be made within one year after the completion of the
survey, and for that purpose plans of the survey shall be
deposited with the Resident Superintendent as soon
as they are approved by the Department of Crown
Lands and shall be open to the inspection of
all Indians entitled to make selections
as aforesaid.

Should

Government

signify

wishes   shall

be

deposited

Crown

Indians

Manitoulin Island shewing (*sic*) portion ceded, 1862

Auguste Kohler, 1862

This is also what
will soon happen on our dear
Manitoulin where only a fifth of their island
remains for the natives, the rest having been
taken away in spite of the rights of the people and
the sacred treaties. The two largest villages (after Holy
Cross) where we had well-built chapels with a house for the
missionary are going to be abandoned. The residents shall no
longer have the right to settle there, nor to choose the mouths
of rivers or ports where the Whites can make settlements for
their residence. Each head of a family shall have one hundred
acres of land and all male children more than ten years of age,
fifty acres. They have been given one year to choose a new
site where they must collect together. I truly do not know
where they will find it, except by occupying swamps
and rocks, as the island is covered with lakes,
one of which is five leagues long and one
third [of the land] is no good
for farming.

Father Superior Auguste Kohler,
surprised to learn that
a Treaty had been concluded.
"Highway robbery,"
he told the government.

also

having

the

longer

settlements

know

rocks   island

long and
good

concluded

Petition to the Government, June 1866

Ottawa (Manitoulin)
Island, Wikwemikong. 18th June 1866.
Thou, Great Chief, We put this on paper in thy
presence, to make known to thee our grievances; how
that Agent at Manitowaning who has the care of us, treats
us. We do not want him, we don't want to have him for Agent.
(for the following reasons)
1. When we go to him (for business) he does not let us enter in his
house but send us somewhere else, because he is proud. Where shall I
learn wisdom? doubtless from he that hates me shall give me wisdom?
He (that Agent) who hates and despises the Indian!
2. He calls us Americans; this is the name he gives me as an insult.
3. The same (Agent) has sent back (to our village) Kitche Batiss to vex
us, also to excite some riot among us, and to have a pretext to send
to Jail our Chiefs. He always works to make us miserable. (We
will never have any more to do with him.) He renders
us no service.
We beseech thee to use thy power to remove
that Dupont (the Agent). This is what
we humbly beg of thee.

We take occasion to
Protest again and to represent to Thee,
how displeased we were, when the Ottawa
(Manitoulin) Island was surrendered, and how we grieve
yet for it. What took place then (the Treaty) was not right at all.
We repeat again now, that we want our Land. Please to the Great
Spirit, that we may own it yet. It does not look well (right) to sell it since
it is only by intimidation that our Land has been taken (from us). Although
we have protested, written to thee until now even, that Thou wouldst destroy
(stop) the sale (of our Land).

It was on October the 4th (to use the English calculation) 1862, that one great Chief
(a commissioner) Wm. McDougall came to speak and made use of some Indians, to
ask them their Lands. But they all refused (loved their Lands) on that day.
It was on October 6th 1862 that some Indians having been spoken to again, and
when they had been intimidated, then only they answered (surrendered the Land).
(The Indians) were not all pleased. Some few Chiefs only (did the thing). But the
majority (a very great number) were not willing at all, and are not yet even now.

We hope that when Thou shall see (know) how things (the Treaty) took place,
it will suggest to thee some great determination. For, indeed we are very
sorrowful for the loss of our Land, and truly we grieve much in our
hearts. We shall never forget it (our Land).

Therefore we humbly beseech Thee, as the Great Chief,
and as the one who loves honestly (right) to
hasten to destroy (to stop) that fraud.
We subscribe our names.

May 29, 1872, William Plummer, Manitowaning Indian Agent, to Joseph Howe, Secretary of State

re lot 28 ...
there is a valuable mill site,
and an Indian clearing. I have the
honour to recommend that a portion
of these lots be reserved for a mill,
or for manufacturing purposes, and as
there is a good harbour for steamers and
vessels, that in addition to the mill-site
Reservation, a sufficient quantity of
land be reserved for
a village plot.

Manitoulin Superintendant J.C. Phipps, November 15, 1873, Manitowaning, to Deputy Superintendant of Indian Affairs William Spragge Regarding Magawong (Kagawong)

I have
visited the Indian village
of Magawong and beg to report that
the Indians have all left the place, and from
the appearance of their deserted gardens, which
are overgrown with brush from four to five feet high,
they do not appear to have been cultivated for several years.
There are but two houses now – one has been occupied ... until
recently, the other is out of repair and unoccupied. The owners
of the houses will probably require some compensation for them
when they learn that the land has been sold, one house is worth ten
dollars, the others out of repair not more than five dollars. There
is an Indian Burial ground covering nearly one quarter of an acre
which should be reserved, as also should be the right of way by
the Indian Trail to Lake Kagawong which passes through the
lot. With these exceptions I would respectfully submit that
it is unnecessary to reserve any portion of Lot No 28 in
the 16th concession of the Township of Billings for
the use of the Indian village of Magawong,
which has been abandoned.

and

and

are

are

an Indian Burial ground covering nearly one quarter of an acre
which should be reserved, as also should be the right of way by
the Indian Trail to Lake Kagawong

has

William Spragge to J.C. Phipps, November 27, 1873

re your
letters of 6th and
16th inst representing that
the Indians do not at present reside
upon lots 27, 28, & 29 in sixteenth con
of the township of Billings (known as the
village of Megawong) I have to inform you
that as their absence thereupon may not
be permanent [except for one family,
they being away at the fishing
grounds] ... provide sketch of
land and determine their
locations.

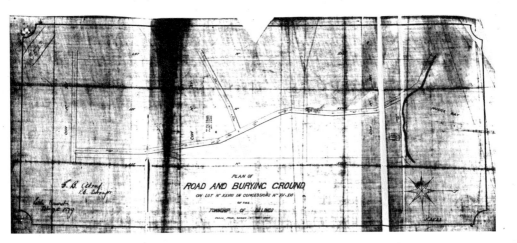

Surveys and Plans: "Indian Trail" and Burying Ground, 1879

2023:
The burial ground is
not demarcated, preserved, or
acknowledged. From the earlier survey
map, it appears the settler graveyard is
layered on top of the "Indian" burial ground.
Lot 28 runs from the shoreline of the bay, the
west side of the River mouth, and alongside
a section of the current River trail. The trail
likely overlays a section of the original
"Indian Trail." Beyond the falls there
is no public access along the
upper-River shoreline.

Simon J. Dawson, Member of Parliament for Manitoulin and the District of Algoma, Speaking of the 1862 Manitoulin Island Treaty in Parliament, 1886

Of
all the
treaties which white
men have made with the
Indians, I believe that it was the
very worst treaty as regards the
Indians ... [it was] most unjust in its
provisions [and] resulted in the
downright robbery [by paying
just $1.79 per head per year
compensation].

Remains of Henry Brothers' mill in Kagawong, at Bridal Veil Falls, 1900–1910

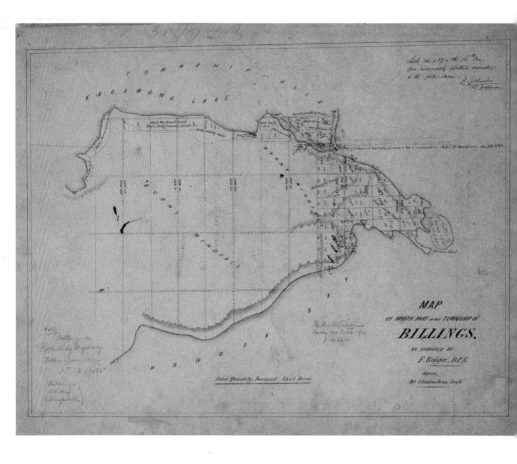

Plan of the North Part of the Township of Billings, 1916

How to Produce the Kagawong River

1. mix mortar and joules
   bury the dead in diseased layers (reshape the shallows)
   muffle the echo of gunshot

2. tramp down the understory with bovine wanderings
   fell the prime timber (follow the flows of capital made natural)
   construct "Nature," remake the River, recreate

3. magnify by five hundred the flagella of colonial desire
   add phosphorus to the calcified claims of zebra mussels
   subtract the everyday from the tourism index (sound back)

4. put down the harvesting baskets
   (put down the harvester), displace the steward
   invest in short root systems and long roads

5. veil the River with the sightlines of subsumed motion
   wed yourself to *Robert's Rules*
   girdle desire (which is your power) in the shape of a River

6. hush the River talking behind the narrowed dam
   ban night walks and unofficial meetings
   silence sovereignty (keep to the approved path)

7. seven is where the ecology should be

Submersion

Geography has a fraught history.
I want to riffle   dominant relations to the River.
Wading into the River   listening   requires submersion within her history.
The body and the   representation,   eyes are not entirely capable of
perceiving long-term   scientific observation,   change, the erasures and hidden
stories, the violence   collections, tools for war,   of maps, the weight of heavy
metals. I must also   imperialism, categorization,   converse with historical
plaques, archival   mapping, power,   materials, garbage cans. The
process of writing   extraction,   moves between the River and the
page, the visual   resource   and the word, the boundaries fluid.
I work across and   through disciplines, struggling
with disciplinary boundaries, and what constitutes
meaning-making. Writing, too, has its own claims.
How might the River write, edit, redact and
re/direct writing, especially about
herself?

Gaagigewang Historical Plaques

For years Manitoulin has been a centre for Anishinaabe artistic production and a stronghold of Anishinaabemowin. Currently, Anishinaabemowin on Manitoulin Island is a threatened language; the vast majority of school age children do not speak it, in fact the majority of Anishinaabeg under the age of fifty-five do not speak Anishinaabemowin. The First Nations of Manitoulin have undertaken a multitude of responses to language shift but with little significant, enduring, wide-ranging success. Local and regional education regimes have demonstrably increased Anishinaabemowin literacy rates, with many second-language learners and fluent speakers engaging and using Anishinaabemowin on social media. However, more resources are required, especially resources that deliberately adopt a decolonial position that seeks to reveal historic truths and uncover toponyms while celebrating and promoting various Anishinaabe achievements in Anishinaabemowin. Grassroots community public art initiatives, like the Kagawong River project spearheaded by sophie, share the spotlight by showcasing Anishinaabe history, Anishinaabe continued presence, Anishinaabe language, and Anishinaabe artistic practice, alongside mainstream public art initiatives.

The Kagawong River project made deliberate attempts to merge artistic interventions while privileging Anishinaabe history, delivering the message trilingually. One aspect of the project was the development of a series of historical plaques that highlighted Anishinaabeg history on Mnidoo Mnising. Out of necessity, the text for the plaques was conceived and written in English, and then translated into French and Anishinaabemowin. A team of three Elders (Alvin Corbiere, Lewis Debassige, Evelyn Roy), along with Clarice Pangowish and I (all of us from M'Chigeeng First Nation), were commissioned to translate those texts. Translating English concepts into Anishinaabemowin challenged the Anishinaabe speaking Elders and made them think hard. The process involved struggling with English, suggesting words, laughing, rejecting, arguing, modifying, and finally, agreeing on the phraseology of the public art and history texts. The process resulted in a product conceived in English and moulded into Anishinaabemowin, a process that seems to echo what is happening with many individual Anishinaabeg who are not fluent – they are grappling with English concepts (as evident on social media) and trying to conceptualize and translate those into Anishinaabemowin. The process undertaken by the Kagawong River Project is instructive for individuals and other grassroots groups – they can replicate it, plant it in other gardens, and watch it grow and flourish.

As many First Nations people try to revitalize their original languages, assistance is required – human and financial. Visual and audio space also needs to be made so that Anishinaabe voices can be heard and their art and literature seen. Many First Nations people also strive to make Anishinaabe-mowin an official language in their respective Territories – this will take assistance, initiative, and persistence from non-Indigenous allies. Hopefully, all across Anishinaabe-akiing (Anishinaabe Territory) many non-Indigenous allies in towns, villages, and cities will also engage in these types of projects, and maybe Anishinaabemowin will get stronger and rejoin Anishinaabe art in visibility and stature. Each time I visit Gaagigewang Ziibi, I am glad to see our language on the Gaagigewang Trail, and I am happy to see it replicated in this book, where people can spend more time with the translations and understand our history in relation to the history of the River included in this book, alongside sophie's creative explorations of River relations. The book supports our efforts at language revitalization and will make our plaque translations more visible and accessible to language learners and simultaneously build more awareness about our history on Mnidoo Mnising.

—**Dr. Alan Ojiig Corbiere**
M'Chigeeng First Nation and York University

Billings Township Connections Trail Plaques, Indigenous History Series

GAAGIGEWANG TOPONYMY

Anishinaabeg (Odaawaag,
Ojibweg, Boodewaadmiig) gii-dnakiiwag
maanpii nikeyiing Mnidoo-Mnising Miinwaa
Nemaanakiki, Gaagigewang, Michigiwadinong Gchi-zhaazhi
jibwaa-dgoshnowaad giwi megwenyig. Gii-mkigaade gaa-bmi-
daawaagbne miinwaa gaa-bi-nakaazwaajin miinwaa aankeyaajmowinan
gkendaagdoon enwek go naa mdaaching mdaaswaak nso-bboon gii-
dnokiiwaagbne Anishinaabeg maanpii Mnidoo-Mnising. Niibwi-Aagwiingwebzowin
nbiish bngising (gakaabikaang) giiwta'iinh gii-zhi-gkendaagwod gonda Anishinaabeg
gaa-bi-dnokiijig Gaagigewang, mii dash wi edming aabjiwang (pane awang) maage
awanbiisaamgad nbiish bi-nji-bngising. Gaa-kidgobne go naa gewii go maaba M'chigeeng
gchi-nishnaabe Ernest Debassige-ba, Gaagigewang nikekmig gii-gchi-piitendaanaawaa
gii-gchi-mnidoo piitendaagwad. Gii-ni-dgwaad'daan dash go wi pii Naadweg gii-bi-
dnaapnazwaad wa Odaawaa jiiskiiwinini Maswe'in gii-dbinooshin shkweyaang nbiish
bngising dbishkoo go naa kawaabid miinwaa dbaajmatwaad mnidoon. Kidownagad
wi ngoding go giizhgag wi pii ndawenjged oodi Gaagigewang, Maswe'in gii-bi-
mgoshkwaan mnidoon oodi ekwaa'ii mshkodeng, gii-kwejmigoon dash wii-
gwejiiyaanaad. Mii dash wi pii gii-pagnaad mnidoon mtakmig, mii mnidoo
gii-ngonaagzid, mdaamni-miinkaanensan miinwaa kosmaani-miikaanensan
gii-ni-njigdaanan waa-naabshkaagjin dbishkoo go naa miingowewzin
niwi Odaawaan. Gtigewin gchinendaagwad Odaawaa gaa-bi-
zhi-bmaadziwaad, dbishkoo gewii gii-bi-giigoonkeng,
ndawenjigeng miinwaa meshkdoongeng.

The Anishnaabeg
(Odaawaa, Ojibwe, and Pottawatomi)
occupied this part of Manitoulin Island including
Maanakiki (Maple Point), Gaagigewang (Kagawong), and
Michigiwadinong (M'Chigeeng) long before European settlers
arrived. Archeological and oral evidence has established at least
10,000 years of Indigenous occupation on Mnidoo Mnising (Manitoulin
Island). The Bridal Veil Falls area was known by Anishinaabe residents as
Gaagigewang (Kagawong), which translates as "always foggy" or "where falling
water throws a mist." According to the late M'Chigeeng First Nation Elder Ernest
Debassige, the Bridal Veil Falls area was a special spiritual place. He related that
during the time of the Iroquois raids the Odaawaa magician Maswein sheltered behind
the Falls, acting as a sentinel and communing with the mnidoog (spirits). Legend has
it that one day when hunting in the Kagawong woods, Maswein came upon a mnidoo
(spirit) at the edge of an open plain and was invited to wrestle. Maswein threw mnidoo
to the ground, and mnidoo disappeared, but corn grains and squash seeds were left in his
place as a gift to the Odaawaa. Agriculture became an important part of Odaawaa culture,
as were fishing, hunting, and trade.

Maankiki
oodenwens Anishinaabe
noowin mii nongo Maple Point
maankikiing maage ni-naatigokiing ezhnikaadeg.
Wemtigoozhwag miinwaa daaweninwag gewiinwaa
gii-zhinkaadana'aa Point aux Erables (Maple Point) Ogima
Baataadagwishkang miinwaa wiiji-anishinaaben gii-daawag akiing
aabtawi'iinh Maanakikiing miinwaa Kaggewang jibwaa-shkwaangeng 1862.
Njida gonaa wda-oodenwensmiwaa mii wi Maanakiki, Gitgaanesmiwaan
gii-yaana'aan gidaaki waabnong nikeyaa Kaggewang zaag'igning miinwaa
ziizbaakdokaan waabnong nikeyaa makomii zaag'igan. Pahtahdagwishkang
gii-mzinbii'aan oodedeman gnoozhen gaa-shkwangeyaad 1862. Gaa-shkwaa
shkwangeyaad, endaajig Maanakikiing, dbishkoo gonaa niibna aanind Anishinaabeg,
gii-nmi-gaazwag gii-aansijgaazwag waa-aawnagbaniin bi-shki-dnokiijig
oodenwensan, nokiiwnan wii-temgag maage jiimaanan e-pangjibdeg miinwaa
gii-aandkiigaazwaad Anishinaabeg nowanj e-gaachngin shkwangaansan.
Ogimaa Pahtahdagwishkung miinwaa niibna niwenh wiiji-anishinaabeman
gii-aanjiwag e-pnishmog Ombidjiwang (Lake Wolsey) wiikji-toowaad
wii-nchikiwziwaad.

The Anishinaabe
name for today's Maple Point
was Maanakiki (forest of maples) or
Nemaanakikong (a point or cape with maple or
hardwood). The French and traders called it Point aux
Érables (Maple Point). Ogimaa (chief) Pahtahdagwishkung
[Baataadagwishkang] and his people lived on the land between
Maanakiki and Lake Kagawong prior to the treaty of 1862. Their
main village was at Maanakiki, their gardens were on the upper
east side of Lake Kagawong, and a sugar bush was east of Ice Lake.
Pahtahdagwishkung signed his fish clan (likely pike) symbol on
the 1862 treaty. After the treaty, the residents of Maanakiki, like
many other island Anishinaabeg, were removed from potential
settler villages, mill sites, or harbours, and resettled in compact
communities or reserves. Chief Pahtahdagwishkung and
many of his people moved west to Ombidjiwang on Lake
Wolsey, trying to remain independent.

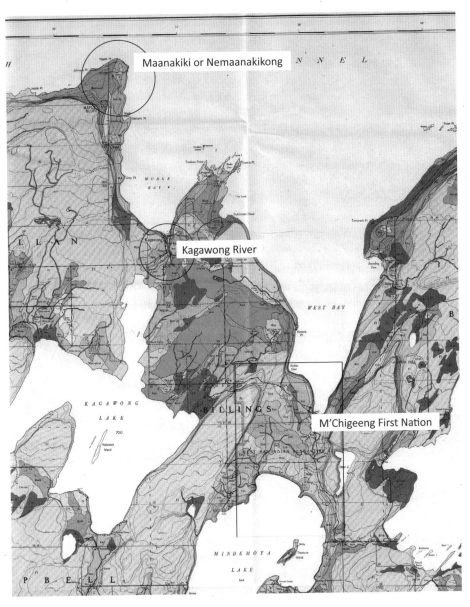

Historical villages of Maanakiki, Gaagigewang, and M'Chigeeng First Nation

Anishinaabe
ednakiijig mii gewii
gnimaa gii-zgaknaanaawaadig
mnoomin besha wiikwedoonsing. Niibna
Anishinaabe ezhi-ngodoodemwaad ensa-ngo-
bboon gii-aandoodegziwaad wii-ziisbaakdakewaad, wii-
zgaknigewaad, ndawenjigewaad miinwaa giigoonkewaad.
Maanda nike'yiinh dnakiiwin miinwaa aki ezhi-nakaazang,
gaawii gii-ngadendziinaa giwi megwenyig. Mii gaa-zhi-
waabndamwaad bmiyaawaad go eta go, gaawii gii-nmetoosiiwag
Anishinaabeg gaa-bmi-dnakiiwaad. Mii maa gaa-nzikaamgad,
mii'sh maa ndinmawaad nendmigoowaad bzhishgoong ki, gaa-
naadmaagwaad mii dash wi wiinwaa gaa-zhi-debwewendmawaad
wii-bi-dnakiiwaad gonda megwenyig. Miinwaa gii-zhi'goomi
gii-shkonmaagoomi bngii akiinsan miziwe Mshiikenh-mnising,
mii go gewii 1862 McDougall Treaty waawiindmaadwin
gaa-nsaaknamaagaazjig Mnidoo-mnising
giwi megwenyig.

Many Anishinaabe
families made regular annual
migrations to long-established
seasonal settlements for sugaring,
harvesting, hunting, and fishing. This type
of settlement and land use was unfamiliar to
Europeans and was interpreted as either nomadic
or lack of evidence of Anishinaabe settlement.
This idea of terra nullius (empty lands) helped to
form the rationale for European occupation and
treaties throughout North America, including
the 1862 McDougall Treaty that opened
Manitoulin to European settlers.

ANISHINAABEG TRADING AND FISHING

Gchi-mewzha Mnidoo-
Mnising Anishinaabeg gii-bmishkaawag
wiigwaas-jiimaaning dkamshkaawaad Mnidoo-
Mnising niibna zaagida-wiikwedong miinwaa zaag'ignan.
Pii ngoji 1830s Anishinaabeg endaajig maanpii pane gii-
bi-nbwaach'igwan daawewininwan gii-taadwag giigoonmiwaan,
ninaatigo-ziisbaakwad, miinwaa mkindaagnan. Gewiinwaa dash swii go
ndawenjgewninwag miinwaa niihgewninwag gii-bmi-ntaa-zhaawag giiwednong
gaaming wii-meshkdoonmaagewaad mkindaagnan. Giigoonkewninwag gii-
zgaknaawaan giigoonyan gbe-bboon maa wiikwedoong Gaagigewang Ziibing miinwaa
Gaagigewang zaag'igning wii-daawewaad miinwaa shandzowaad. Pii 1860 Anishinaabeg
endaajig maampii gii-ginjgaaazwag nchiwaad niizhtana ninwag ooshme mdaaswi-shi-niiwin
endsa-bboongizjig, miinwaa niizhtana mackinaw ezhnikaadegin jiimaanan. Weweni go gii-
gkendaagwad giigoonke danakiiwin bezhig jiimaan endsa-bezhig giigoonke-winini. Kina Billings
eshki-dgoshnowaad megwenyig Mnidoo-Mnising shkode-jiimaaning gii-bi-yaawag, mii'sh
miinwaa egaaching bemaasing jiimaan maage Mackinaw jiimaaning biinish Gaagigewang.
Mii'sh gegpii gii-ni-bmosewaad wdakiinsmiwaang. Mackinaw jiimaanan gii-bi-nzikaanoon
Anishinaabeg wiigwaas-jiimaanwaan miinwaa bemaasing jiimaan, gaa-nakaazang gchi-gmiing.
Nowanj go gii-gzhiibdenoon wiigwaas-jiimaanan, gaa dash wii go gii-waankiiwendaagsinoon
wii-bmaasing. Dbishkoo wiigwaas-jiimaanan, Mackinaw-jiimaanan naamya'ii gii-
nbagaanoon, (neniidweyiinh) e'edweyiinh gii-giinkojiiyaanoon, gii-wenpandoon
wii-gwaabjigaadeg. Eni-shkwaaseg dash go wi mkindaagni-meshkdoongewin, mii
nonda giigoonke-jiimaanan gii-bi-aawang. Megwenyig miinwaa Anishinaabeg gii-
nakaaznaawaa biinish 1940s, jibwaa-miigaading.

For centuries Manitoulin
Anishinaabeg travelled by canoe across
Manitoulin's countless external bays and inland lakes. By
the 1830s Anishinaabe residents here were visited regularly by
traders who competed for fish, maple sugar, and furs. Though hunters and
trappers usually travelled to the north shore for furs, fishermen harvested fish
year-round in the bay, the Kagawong River, and Kagawong Lake to sell and to feed
their families. In 1860 the Anishinaabe residents here were recorded as having twenty
males over fourteen years of age and twenty Mackinaw fishing boats. It was clearly a fishing
community – a boat for every man. All of Billings' early settlers arrived on Manitoulin by
steamboat, then travelled by small sail or Mackinaw boat to Kagawong, and finally overland
to their lots. Mackinaw boats evolved from the First Nation peoples' canoes, a hybrid of
traditional canoe and European sailboat constructions. Canoes could travel quickly but were
unstable with a mast and sail. Like canoes, Mackinaw boats were flat-bottomed, double-
ended, and could be hauled ashore. As the fur trade declined these boats became fishing
boats and were known to be used by local residents and First Nations
members until the early 1940s.

Maanda gchi-wiikwed,
mii Anishinaabeg gchi-namtoowin
ni-dgosing ziibiin, zaag'ignan, dkamoojiignan
miinwaa wiikwedoon ni-zgamag oodenawensing. Gii-
mnwaabndaanaawaa gonda megwenyig, gewiinwaa Anishinaabeg
gaa-bmi-namtoowaad gaa-zhi-mnawaabndamwaad wii-wenpanziwaad
bmakzhwewaad nbiing bmiyaang bmoodegzing gii-gchi-piitendaagwad
megwenyig bi-dnakiijig. Gaagigewang-wiikwed aapji go gii-gchi-nendaagwad
gaa-zhi-giigoonkaamgag Anishinaabeg gaa-nji-giigoonkewaad. Mnidoo-Mnising
Anishinaabeg gii-giigoonkewag giiwtaagmi miinwaa gii-meshkdoonaawaan
giigoonyan jibwaa-naaknigaadeg miinwaa gii-mzinignikaadeg maaba Gchi-gimaa
1859. Nonda giigoonke-mzin'ignan gii-dgishkaanaa'aa Anishinaabeg,
gii-debwewendmoog gii-nagamigaazwaad dbendmowaad kina maanda nikekmig
miinwaa giiwtaagmi maaba Bond Head gaa-zhi-waawiindmaaged 1836.
Endagmoojgejig miinwaa begdawaajig gii-bshigendaagwad maanpii 1880s.
Nongo giigoonskeng, gndamoojgeng maazhmegos geyaabi go nooj'aan
bemaadzinjin Gaagigewang, Mchigiing miinwaa go
aanind oodenawensan.

Mudge Bay was part of
a vast Anishinaabe transportation
system involving rivers, lakes, portage
trails, and bays connecting Island communities
to the North Shore and Lake Huron. The network was
embraced by early settlers who appreciated the value of
water transportation, as it was critical to settlement and
transportation of goods. Mudge Bay was an important fishing
ground for the original Anishinaabe residents who fished
these waters and traded fish long before fishing was regulated
and licensed by the government in 1859. These licences were
opposed by the Anishinaabeg, who believed they had been
acknowledged as proprietors of the region's land and waters
by the Bond Head Treaty of 1836. Later, c1880, sport and
commercial fishing became popular here. Today, smelting,
sport fishing, and salmon continue to attract people
from Kagawong, M'Chigeeng First Nation, and
other communities.

GOVERNMENT CLAIMS

1836 Anishinaabeg
debendngig Mnidoo Mnis miinwaa Gchi-
gimaa gii-beshaakbii'aanaawaa waawiindmaage-
mzinigan. Wi zhaagnaashii-mzinigan weweni wiindmaagemgad
wi neniizh gii-giizhaaknigewaad ji-zhenmawaawaad ji-mshkomwaad
niwi mnishensan kina dash Anishinaabeg ji-dnakiiwaad maa pane. Mii
dash wi 1862 gchi-gimaa naagaanzijig gii-zhitoonaawaa bkaan naaknigewin
wi Anishinaabeg, gaawii gii-de-nchisiiwag maa Mnidoo-Mnising. Miinwaa
gewiinwaa gii-mkawaataanaawaa wi gaa-aanjbiigaadeg waawiindmaage-
mzinigan ji-bgidnaazwaapa megwenyig ji-dnakiiyaapa, ji-maajiishkaatoowaapa
bmiiwziwnan miinwaa nakiiwnan zhiwi Mnidoo-Mnising. Gaa-bi-zhiwebag maa gii-bi-
beshaakbiigaadeg wi waawiindmaage-mzinigan 1862, geyaabi go dbaaddemgad nongo
maanda giizhgag. Billings miinwaa Allan dnakiiyaansan miinwaa Gaagigewang oodenwens
gii-maajiishkaajgaade niwi zhaazhi kiinsan Nemaankiki, Gaagigewang miinwaa
Michigiwadnong Anishinaabeg. Mii go kina gewii ngoji gaa-bmi-zhi-zhiwebag Canada
(Kanadaa), gaa-bmi-shkwaa-zhiwebag dash shkwaach gii-beshaakbiigeng bidgosing
gii-daapnigaazsigwaa miinwaa gii-aandanakiigaazwaad Anishinaabeg maa nji
gaa-maajiishkaatoowaajin bmiiwziniwaan miinwaa ednakiiwaad. Mii dash
wdikdownan Mnidoowaaning dzhi-mekdekwanye Zhaabens (Jabez) Sims
1867: "Da-nakiiwinan maa mnising gonda Myegwenyig, gaawii gii-
mno-daapnaasiiwaan Anishinaaben wii-mno-maajiishkaanid."

In 1836 the Anishnaabeg
proprietors of Manitoulin Island
signed an agreement with the Crown. The
English text clearly stated that they both agreed to
withdraw their claims to the islands, making them the
property for all "Indians" to reside thereon. However, in 1862
government officials made an unusual claim that the Anishnaabeg
had not populated Manitoulin sufficiently. They also brought forward
a revised treaty that would allow European settlers to establish
businesses and communities on Manitoulin Island. The circumstances
under which the Treaty of 1862 was signed remain controversial to this
day. Billings and Allan Townships and Kagawong village were established
on the former lands of the Maanakiki, Gaagigewang, and Michigiwadinong
Anishnaabeg. As was true in many parts of Canada, the aftermath of the
last treaty signing included the disenfranchisement and displacement
of Anishnaabeg from their established businesses and communities.
In his 1867 report to the Society of the Propagation of the
Gospel, Manitowaning resident Rev. Jabez Sims wrote, "The
settlement of the Island by the whites has operated
very much against the interests of the Indians."

CHANGES TO THE RIVER

Gaagigewang
ziibi ni-piichi-aansemgad;
Niibna go maanda enji-aansemgag. Mii
dash wi nji gaa-bi-shki-dnakiijig miinwaa ki gaa-
bi-zhi-nakaazwaad. Anishinaabeg njida gaa-daajig gii-
giigoonkewag miinwaa gii-zgaknaanaawaa e-zaagkiig maa ziibing
miinwaa giiwtaayiing kiing, wi pii ziibi gii-aansemgag, mii wi nji pane go
naa ezhi-aandkamgisemgag. Gaa-bi-shki-dnakiijig megwenyig gii-mtigkewag
wii-dinmowaad waa-nakaazwaad wii-zhigewaad. Mtigoog gii-gwiboojgaazwag,
gii-daashkboozgaazwag waa-naabjikaazang wii-zhigeng, ni-dbasaakwaa, mii dash wi
gaa-ni-nji-maajiiyaaboodeg tib-ziibi. Mii dash ni-aanjiiyaamgag ezhayaamgag maanda
ziibi. Megwenyig gii-nendaagziwag wii-dwaakwemawaad kiin gaa-nji-mshkamwaad,
gii-miingaazwag mnik waa-njitaa'aad; nonda gchi-niibna gaa-mzhiiyaakwegaadegin gii-
ndinegemgad niibna nbiish wii-maajiiyaajwang.gaa-shki-maajtaamgad Billings dnakiiyaansan,
bzhikoog gii-paabaasjigewag pime-ziibing. Mii dash miinwaa bnaadkamgaa'gewag
bnaajtoonaawaa bjiinag bi-dba'kiig. Gmaapiich dash go gtigeng ndingemgad washme waa-ni-
pichiyaamgag paabwan gaa-ni-zhijwang nbiing. Gaa-zhichgaadegin bgashkboojganan miinwaa
daashkboojganag gii-aandaajwan nbiish ezhjiwang miinwaa gbaakwigaadeg ziibi wipii 1874,
miinwaa'sh go bekish waasmowin zhichgaadeg, miinwaa naabkinigan zhichgaade, ziibiikaajgan wii-
zhijwang enji-zhichgaadeg waasmowin, gii-aanjtoonaawaa mnik bemjiwang miinwaa ezhjiwang
nbiish eni-baashkjijwang miinwaa eni-zhijwang, giiwtaa-ziibi. Washme dash naanoomye
bekaanzijig shka'yaag noonj e-nsweyaangizjig gii-gtigaazwag njida go (maazhnmegos), miinwaa
dash go giwi gaa-giimooj-dgoshngig ('Rusty' zhaagenjgaansag miinwaa 'zebra' esiinsag).
Maamig gaa-maajiishkaajgaazjig taadwag e-maawnji-nshid mii go maanpii njida enjibaajig.
Wii-gshkitoong waa-zhi-naagdawendming e-kwiindmaamgag, ezhjiwang, epiichjiwang
miinwaa wii-bwaa-nshinaadag, Billings naagaanzijig ni-dgobzowag Mnidoo Mnising
ziibiin wii-naandwechgaade maanda ziibi.

The Kagawong River has changed
over time; much of this change is closely linked to
the history of settlement and land-use patterns. The original
Anishinaabe residents fished and harvested plants from the River and
surrounding lands, but changes to the River then were primarily due to natural
ecological shifts. The settlement patterns of Europeans included harvesting timber
to supply the growing demand for building materials. Timber was felled to supply the
mill and for construction, reducing the overstory, contributing to erosion of the Riverbanks,
and changing the ecology of the River. Settlers were required to clear claimed lands within a
certain period of time; these large deforested areas contributed to increased water run-off. In
the early years of Billings' settlement, cattle grazed along the Riverbanks, eroding the ground and
impacting the understory. Over time agriculture has contributed to increased levels of phosphates
in the local watershed. The creation of the grist and saw mills changed water flow, and the damming
of the River in 1874, along with power generation and the building of the canal to feed the power
plant, changed both the quantity and direction of water flow over the falls and along the
River. Over the years new species have been introduced, intentionally (such as salmon) and
unintentionally (including the rusty crayfish and zebra mussels). These, along with new
hybrids, are competing with indigenous species.

Historical Plaques, Remix

History is not as clean as edited plaques. I randomly cut a line from the text of each of the thirty-five settler and Indigenous plaques. The phrases reset uneasily against each other like the settler bones layered on top of the Indigenous ones at the cemetery along the River.

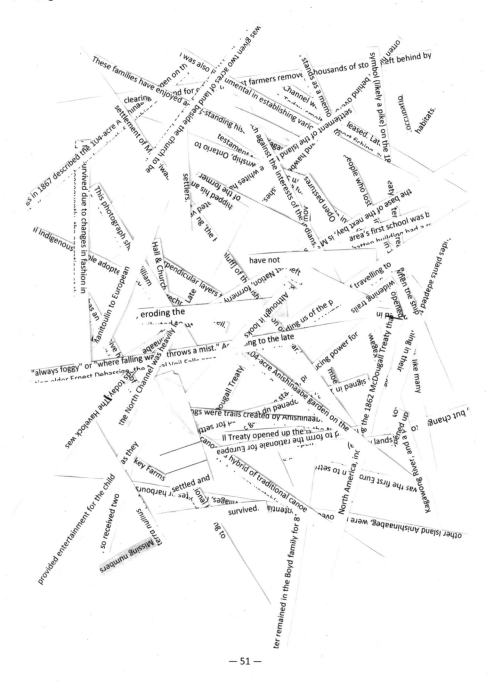

Historical Plaques, Remix Two

here they were are
the spot
re-collection: lines and paths become single points
map: (power of)
time made
static
memory

is
under
foot
layer the bones
turn (flint, shard) back under the soil
(the truth beats its wings against the purple-lighted panes)
our good intentions (legal advice required)
allow "displace," once
the ( ) gaps
in a settler archive
admit ( )

no
loss ( )
place (our noun)
pin (your verbs)
consider this (maple-sugar basket, mackinaw boat) (motorboat)
representative
we look at history as though
through a
thirty-five-image
view
finder

January 5
zhiishiibak, ducks

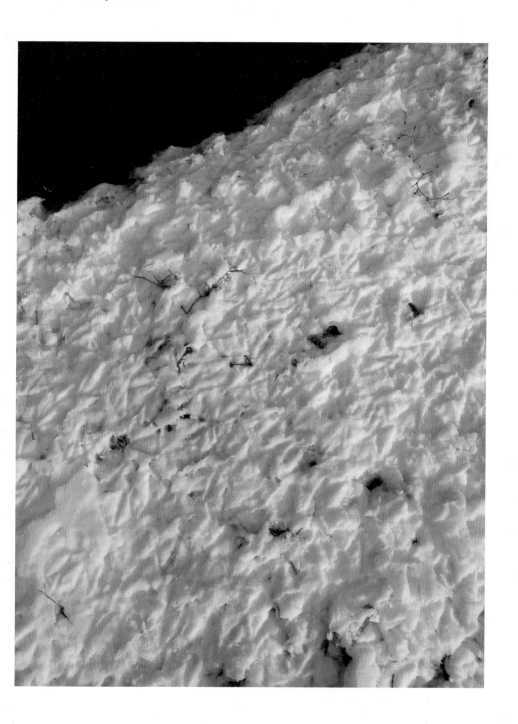

February 13
305 Steps in Snow at Hip Height

GRAPHITE SUSPENDED OVER PAPER IN A BOX STRAPPED TO MY BODY

shpaagnagaa, be deep snow
aagmak, snowshoes

My body moves through the River returned as snow. I move through the trees.
My body writes its tracks, its lines on the ground, through the air. The body is motion.
Language is motion. I want to shift from the stasis of the written text, to write in the
way that the River's ecosystem is always in process. The way that Anishinaabemowin
is so verb based, less noun oriented than English, a mobile language. I hang a box from
my shoulders, over which graphite is suspended, moving freely as my body moves. My
daughter Emilie is with me, we laugh as we struggle through the hip-high snow, the box
recording my motion onto paper. This is my first experiment along the Kagawong River.

February 15

THE WIND AND A SPRUCE TREE ALONG THE KAGAWONG RIVER
COLLABORATING ON A TEXT

bngishwaanmat, be a west wind
gaawaandgwaatik, spruce

I have been wondering what the Gaagigewang Ziibi might say about herself if she
wrote her own plaques and texts.

February 15

THE WIND IN CONVERSATION WITH A BALSAM,
BAAPAASHKWAATIK

February 20

I use a field book to think through my process on the River. I like the language of a fieldbook over that of a sketchbook. The fieldbook helps me bring a critical awareness to my process, yet integrates the highly personal, process-based, and introspective aspects of the sketchbook. The River is not a neutral site out there to be observed and is something of which I am a part. Something which may not be visible, apprehensible, or stable. Listening and observing is a subjective and unstable meaning-making process.

I begin by walking along the River. I am attracted to the embodied and the sensory, but I know I cannot know the River without also understanding how she's become what she's become, and how she continues becoming.

January 20, February 20
Making Tracks

CARDBOARD LETTERS PLACED IN HEAVILY DEER-TRACKED CEDAR STAND NEXT TO THE WATER

bmikwe, leave footprints, leave tracks
ekwishin, an imprint of one be left somewhere, leave an imprint
somewhere, there be an imprint of someone's body somewhere

Over nine months I walk the same track in a straight line along the letters.
I am aware of the claims inherent in the seemingly simple act of walking on
the land and writing about it. How I think influences how I understand where
my feet travel, structures my relationships, reveals how I go about knowing,
and how I write about it.

March 2, Ink on Ice

bbaamkomii, walk around on the ice

We have moved into ice again. Ice pans collect along the River. A sheet of ice has separated and dropped from the bank, leaving an exposed and flat ice surface. I step down onto the detached ice, run my hand along the smooth surface. The lower shelf of ice is creaking and snapping below my feet; it may not be here tomorrow. The ice at the falls has changed dramatically in the last week. With water-based ink, I brush words onto the ice surface. The words I choose do not matter so much as their transformation, the ink seeping, spreading, like tiny root hairs. Translated into a third language, a shared language created between my hand, the ice, and the ink.

MINUTE FIVE

Ink on Ice, Poem 2

MINUTE SIX

March 2

I want to hang three articles that propose axioms for landscape interpretation. It takes a while, but I finally find a spot. I'd thought about submerging them in the River but an earlier attempt to submerge a poem resulted in it being swept away by the current. With other poems being removed by walkers, it is tricky to find somewhere they might avoid being found for a few months.

In the end I tuck the articles up under some cedar branches high in a tree facing the River. I have stitched the three articles together, oldest to newest, with two strips of birchbark for support, and I tie these to the tree. I hide the twine as much as possible with dried cedar branches. I like how they are facing the River, the River looking back.

The three geography texts include the classic and problematic 1979 "Axioms for Reading the Landscape: Some Guides to the American Scene," by Peirce Lewis, which was very influential in the reading of cultural landscapes through observation, and which set the standard for landscape interpretation for several decades; Don Mitchell's 2008 intervention, "New Axioms for Reading the Landscape: Paying Attention to Political Economy and Social Justice," which contributed to spatial justice by expanding Pierce's axioms to a consideration of the invisibilized processes and power that produce landscape; and finally, Jonathan D. Phillips's more recent (2018) article with a geophysical perspective, "Place Formation and Axioms for Reading the Natural Landscape."

Ecology is somehow missing from both earlier papers, yet the geophysical paper is limited in its own way. I want the River and the elements to speak back, want to acknowledge the River as an agent, for her to do her own interpretation, to bring the three papers together, no claim having the final authoritative word. Each is unsettled, moved by the next, and each will give way to the River in the end. Like my own ideas.

March 3, Axioms

THREE LANDSCAPE INTERPRETATION TEXTS HUNG IN A CEDAR TREE FACING THE RIVER

giizhkaandag, cedar tree

March 4

"Seeing comes before words," writes John Berger in *Ways of Seeing*. "It is seeing which establishes our place in the surrounding world; we explain that world with words, but words can never undo the fact that we are surrounded by it. The relation between what we see and what we know is never settled." I am in the process of seeing the River and hearing, touching, and feeling her. Finding ways to listen with all my senses, to explain what I see within the limits of my capacity to hear and write. Trying to find a space between languages. The relation between what I see and what I write is never settled. At what point does a drawing or a handful of letters become a poem?

March 4, Late Afternoon

esbaanh, raccoon

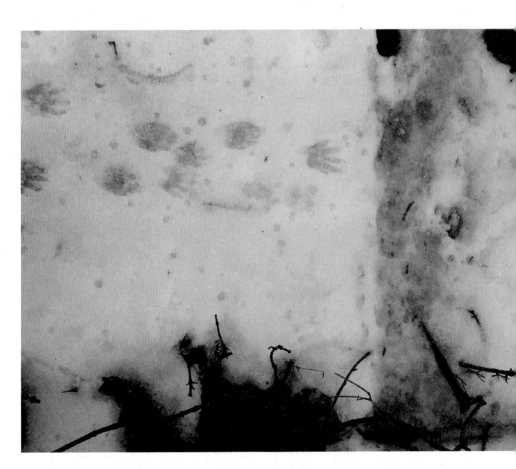

March 5

KINONAAN WAAWAASHKESHWAN, CONVERSATION WITH DEER

jidmoonyik, squirrels
waawaashkesh, deer
zhibii'ganag, alphabet letters

The small fragments of cedar buds dropped by squirrels and birds onto the snow prompt me to drop an alphabet of cardboard letters from a cedar tree growing angled alongside the River. Over the winter, deer walk through the letters on their regular route to the water. The letters are covered by hoof prints and snow, then uncovered, sinking into the melt as the weather warms, becoming submerged as the freshet turns the cedar grove into River. It is a constantly shifting reveal of letters. I climb the cedar regularly to document the process from above.

March 14

March 17

THE WIND IN CONVERSATION WITH A CEDAR

giizhkaandag, eastern white cedar

March 25

We are in another period of change, when winter and spring cohabitate. I am glad for the hardening of the diminishing snow, so that I can snowshoe one last time around the edge of the softening bay. Soon the bush will be hard to navigate. I run my fingers along the soft willow buds. A crow shadows me. My daughter laughs when I repeat the calls of crows, but there are days when these are the only sounds that make sense. When I spend time on the River it is inevitable that I think about transitions – personal, seasonal, ecological, global. There are some transitions that are not seasonally or ecologically normal. I do not know how to advise my daughter in her sleepless nights, as she wonders how to proceed or conceive a life. My poems offer little in the way of what should be typical wisdom, maternal or otherwise. And in this, I feel the limits of poetry.

March 26, Tracks

bmikwaanan, footprints, tracks

My repeated walking over the alphabet through the winter has created an icy path.

April 7

giigdowin, conversation

The conversation is no longer with the deer, but with the freshet.

Spring

mnookmi, be spring, be springtime
mooshk'an, there is a flood, it is flooded
mooshk'an, runoff

Freshet

The River has no mind for the tourist today
she races over the limestone cliff

the walkway is flooded. the spray reaches the
staircase. the green water runs over the muddy edges
of the banks, carries with her lost words, the failed promises
and projects of winter, a section of dock, dog shit, salt, and sand
crumbs dropped from an ice shack in January
released from the melting ice, the nocturnal dreamings
of pimply teenagers, the small bloated body
of a lost hamster, a limp condom
the long twining section of fishing line shorn
from a hook embedded in a sodden snag
streaking phosphorous from up-lake farms
cigarette butts and beer cans, a collection of single mittens
a single red-leather dance shoe dropped over the bridge
on New Year's Eve.

The River ejects herself into the bay
warns, in the single-minded memory of herself: stay back.

April 4

nwiiyaw, my body

The River composes me. The more time I spend on the River,
the more composed I become.
Calm.
Written by. Rewritten.

In January I stepped into the River because of grief, lifted my feet
through the deep snow. The cold emptied then filled me, the way the
scents of spring and the rising water fill my skin. I follow the changes on
the River, but I'm not sure how to trace the changes of the River on me,
on the way I see, hear, and write, to track the relationship of the River
with me on multiple scales. I move beyond senses, beyond the body,
and back again. Time changes the conversation. There is desire, but no
linear way to write the desire to walk here, to proceed without drawing
along existing dynamics. There is love that comes from this deepening,
this sinking into the River.

"If a revolt is to come, it will have to come from the five senses!"
—Michel Serres

I want to move into and beyond the sensory, beyond the distillation of
pleasure and the evaporation of grief which the River draws down into
her. Another taking from the River. Yet also a beginning, a translation of
knowledge through skin. I am drawn to wading into the strong spring
current, to loosen and to lose myself in it, to undo the language I know,
make space for words to grow from my green cells. Grow new words
that speak differently, walk with grace through the River and away from
her, into a differently worded world.

April 8

baagnige, strike, flash a lightning bolt

Lightning Strike

how to capture the
blue of black
the bird flies from the
branch blue + black
separate in mid...

April 12

gbe-bboon, all winter
bboon, be winter
mnookmi, be spring
wiinjiishkwaak, be mud

I have been finding birds' nests, zaswinan, throughout this winter and spring – blown from trees, knocked out of branches, dropped into pathways. They are small marvels. The nest of a robin, pichi, with its layer of mud, and a small red-eyed vireo nest woven with birchbark, wiigwaas, and other materials. I am inspired by these weavings and the use of birchbark, which I have also been collecting all winter, picking up the small pieces that I find on my walks. I don't know why I collect. Is this a haunting of nineteenth-century claiming via collecting? A naturalist tendency? Dimensional poetry installed on windowsills, along with deer bones, kanan, fossils, fish scales, a snakeskin, dead flies, a porcupine skull. Mnemonic love.

I am attracted to things that are well-worn. Holes, dead things. The process of change and decay. Gaps and meanderings, marks. My life is full of holes. I am emptying of fullness. I know nothing, again.

I want to write a poem for the nesting birds. I can't find words that would be of any use to a bird.

April 15, Words for Birds

NESTING MATERIAL

bneshiinh, bird

Below the first high bank I watch for birds. A sparrow flies past, landing
on the leaf litter, hops around the base of a poplar, up and over a deadfall.
When it leaves, I plant the words for birds on this mossy fallen tree.

April 18

DEER TRACKS, DAY FORTY-FOUR

At the peak of the freshet, the stand of cedars has become an island. One by one the letters are submerged, all but the letter *B*.

May 5

The branches   reach towards   the River

The River has peaked. Although the snow is gone from the bush, it lies in the deep cracks of the ridge. I somehow expected to be finished with grief by spring, but it is crystalline in the deep places. I continue to be surprised, and surprised by my surprise, by what people will take and claim. There are days when I feel full of holes. I am told I need to speak to and through these textures of taking.

Trauma seeps through the cracks, finds its way like rain. We re/cycle through it. I am stitching my life, recreating myself in this slow process with the River. I call up words and stitch the lines that hold me together. I remind myself that a jagged tear heals better. I am grateful for words, sounds, language: for this lifeline, regardless of how hard it is to find time to write some weeks, and to find words. There are words I have lost, words I can't speak, words I have tried to forget, words I need to reclaim. I walk, I write, I fill my field books. I seek my lost words. Flashes of green poke up through the brown and flattened leaves. Bright-green buds extend the cedar's fingers. The birds are busy flickering past my eyelids along with the sun which flashes between trees and branches. The sounds of the River change from day to day and month to month as the foliage grows and the grasses fill out along the banks.

May 21, Rain poem

bgambiisaa, the rain comes

Using graphite I write a poem on the rocks by the walking bridge that crosses the River below the power station, but the letters are so faint. I will have to go back in the rain and try again. I frighten a couple of walkers who don't see me tucked under the bridge transferring the poem to the rock. They make me jump too, in their surprise.

I have overdressed and drape my sweater and jacket through the bag across my back. I retrace my steps and find my camera-lens cover.

I am glad to have been on the River for a few hours and not to have felt rushed. I like seeing the flyfishers at the mouth of the River. It is all about patience and listening to the water, the elements. They don't talk to each other but talk to the rain and the sun.

I want hip waders so I can spend more time in the cool water.

Long Rainfall

they like me least when   i

gather   in sheets and   crevices

frozen earth   into   cracks   over roadways

under doors

i can't be held i fill the loose weave of sweaters

warmth   of their   skin   i steal the

i refuse to be held

they cannot hold all of me   and when the earth is

dry and cracked nor can   the earth receive me   i skim

over the earth   and its

thirsting roots

to hold me you too must be loose

a veining system

you must lose the illusion of solidity

and stasis   seep into blue you must   fill your lungs and

you too must be loose   or   disintegrated

mere particles

May 22

It is so different on the east bank of the Kagawong. In some ways the human impact is more obvious even though it is quieter on this side of the River: the lack of underbrush, the eroded bank, the coconut fibre protecting the bank from erosion near the mouth of the River. There is a giant ash that has fallen and is full of insect holes. I want to count all the ash trees and map the gaps in the canopy that will develop once the ash borer has done its devastation. I consider attaching a letter and a QR code to each ash with a link to a map, a poem, a death count, a drawing of the canopy.

I wonder if I can join the grass before I die. Become grass and mud. Move beyond the limits of my body. I print a poem and punch holes into the paper. I want to plant it somewhere along the River, where grass might grow up through the words. Push through my edges, the boundaries between human and plant.

May 22, Conversation with the Riparian

ddibew, Riverbank, near water's edge

I have been thinking about the porosity between bodies, exchange. What it might mean to lie in the grasses and be transformed. I plant poems (or they are planting me) on the east and west banks of the River in the riparian border, transitional, filtering space that speaks to this boundary, or rather this crossing or conjoining of boundaries. The riparian, a border between water and land, a filter, harbour, habitat, a liminal border space but also a solidifier, provider of protection and shade, maintaining shoreline stability. The poems / the riparian and / I are not finished.

June 8

Although I began with my field book, I increasingly lift my work off the page. I'm trying to build "relational muscle."

This listening to and with the River, along with the invitation to collaborate, extends the definition of reader, writer, creator along with where and how the work is disseminated, and by whom.

Just as sure as I am that a different sort of human/more-than-human conversation is possible and necessary, I am equally convinced that this process of conversing with the River may be a mere conceit, a limited, tentative, and anthropocentric response to anthropocentrism and the western dominance of nature.

June 20

I walk the trail repeatedly. The River sounds sunny today, the light reflects off the riffles. She is chatty and gregarious as she rushes around the little islands of grasses.

I draw. I leave poems behind. My footsteps, like all the others along the path on the west side of the River, follow and overprint the "Indian trail" that led from the mouth of the River to the upper River, and the gardens that were situated in what is now a tent and trailer park.

I walk more and more slowly, attempt to make the walking uncomfortable.

How to Tell a Geospatial Story

1.   see how the River reshapes herself reshapes herself reshapes herself
around the morphology of limestone (prevailing winds)
read the substrate of slow time, the silt of fast decisions

2.   poplar and poison ivy fill the spaces of harvested hardwoods
the River flows towards biological efficiency
(follow the signs of loss following demands for durability)

3.   like other Rivers, the River emerged as River after the glacial lake
streamed away, here, the limestone is a great lake breath
at the cusp of north and south, sedimentary and shield (pause)

4.   roots slip into the cracks of bare limestone, silt and runoff run
down the high bank, fluvial processes agglomerate
eggs deposit in gravel deposits (parse place)

5.   canalize the River, plot for historical legacies, the weathered
limestone cannot return to being unweathered
weather ongoing evolutions and disturbances (field field notes)

6.   set the clock for a clock-resetting event, do not hold your
breath, there is a threshold for stability and obliteration
(place is reversible) create historically contingent field notes

7.   this is where my heart should be (what is the axiom for silence?)

August 4

I am always surprised
when people don't know
where the falls come from
don't know where the water is going
as though the River appears
at the lip of the   limestone drop

I spend multiple hours over several days sitting at the edge of the pool at Bridal Veil
Falls during the busiest tourist weekend of the year. I have set a lidded wooden box on
another piece of limestone.
In the box are pieces of birchbark found on the ground along the trail, pencils and pens
a notebook, along with an invitation to write something
for or about the River
to send a message
down the River on a piece of birch.

There is something   about waterfalls
that makes a person   simultaneously reverential and giddy
    certain that this is the way   the earth has always
        been and   always will be
unaware of the history of the River   unaware
                that the River has, over time, been diverted
        dammed   filled with mechanical debris.

I imagine the water rising
rising over the banks, rising over the villages.
    Conversely, the water   evaporating
cities barren   I watch these visitors with their faces   turned
        to the falls   full of joy, and I count

I gather the words shared in the notebook.

water supplies shrink temperatures rise precipitation patterns shift. severe storms
degrade wat
survival of r
communitie:
defenses. Rt
grow more fi
of CSOs coul
by lower fl
precipitation
to dilute pol
dissolved ox
ecos
and
expo
ever
as ai
the f
and
poll
path
to b
cons
supp
wate
man
have
from
as e
incr
and
lowe
Higher temp
levels, both
global temp
extreme sto
with temper
Water tempe
rises. lead tc
crustaceans
precipitation
washed into
pesticides, a
to larger boc

my quixotic. honey. i love you more than yesterday less than tomorrow forever and always. may we grow and progress, as the water that flows from these rocks, this history. live your best life. take risks. life is like a river, let it run its course. we are blessed with this waterfall. positive masculinity is shown through grounded certainty. anything can be anything to anyone. cherish feelings, they are the only thing that we know is real. soothing flow, refreshing, renewal. bubbles. my quixotic. honey. i love you more than yesterday less than tomorrow forever and always. may we grow and progress, as the water that flows from these rocks, this history. live your best life. take risks. life is like a river, let it run its course. we are blessed with this waterfall. positive masculinity is shown through grounded certainty. anything can be anything to anyone. cherish feelings, they are the only thing that we know is real. soothing flow, refreshing, renewal. bubbles. my quixotic. honey. i love you more than yesterday less than tomorrow forever and always. may we grow and progress, as the water that flows from these rocks, this history. live your best life. take risks. life is like a river, let it run its course. we are blessed with this waterfall. positive masculinity is shown through grounded certainty. anything can be anything to anyone. cherish feelings, they are the only thing that we know is real. soothing flow, refreshing, renewal. bubbles. my quixotic. honey. i love you more than yesterday less than tomorrow forever and always. may we grow and progress, as the water that flows from these rocks, this history. live your best life. take risks. life is like a river, let it run its course. we are blessed with this waterfall. positive masculinity is shown through grounded certainty. anything can be anything to anyone. cherish feelings, they are the only thing that we know is real. soothing flow, refreshing, renewal. bubbles. my quixotic. honey. i love you more than yesterday less than tomorrow forever and always. may we grow and progress, as the water that flows from these rocks, this history. live your best life. take risks. life is like a river, let it run its course. we are blessed with this waterfall. positive masculinity is shown through grounded certainty. anything can be anything to anyone. cherish feelings, they are the only thing that we know is real. soothing flow, refreshing, renewal. bubbles. my quixotic. honey. i love you more than yesterday less than tomorrow forever and always. may we grow and progress, as the water that flows from these rocks, this history. live your best life. take risks. life is like a river, let it run its course. we are blessed with this waterfall. positive masculinity is shown through grounded certainty. anything can be anything to anyone. cherish feelings, they are the only thing that we know is real. soothing flow, refreshing, renewal. bubbles. my quixotic

threaten the
r overflows.
icture fewer
vs (CSO) will
ie frequency
ompounded
and shifting
ig less water
; and reduce
ant harm to
ncy
ises
ion
oirs
on
e —
ore
ase
end
atic
ter
ade
I of
hat
noff
ent
uld
ows
rns
nts.
ived oxygen
tems. Rising
d severity of
xponentially
s and floods.
temperature
fish, insects,
nore intense
lution to be
pathogens,
to be carried
equences of

heavy runoff can be blooms of harmful algae and bacteria. as precipitation patterns shift

Bridal Veil(ed) Falls

we splash wade cell- and beer-handed lift
faces to spray enraptured giddy   sun-reddened
                              posts   multiply
             i am double   visioned
   see the falls   see falling
        we are caught up   but not in god   caught
             rupture   not rapture
                                                        veiled
             sight
                              blindness

   the sun   limestone   solid under fingers the rushing water the
rock trees
   rooted to the ravine   how is anything other   possible

             married to ghosts we cling to old vows
                                                  constant growth
        consummated   without   synaptical transference

             yellow dog-toothed violet
        blue crystalline breath in december dusk bejeweled
   caddis fly
        unfurling fern pungent leek
what production   worth the gently speaking jack-in-the-pulpit

        it continues
             we continue
                              the hand becoming visible

        can we be   graceful
             midwife the River   while
                         accepting our own possibly
                         necessary fall

        what word   worth
                         the weight of paper

By slow violence
I mean a violence that occurs
gradually and out of sight, a violence of
delayed destruction that is dispersed across time
and space, an attritional violence that is typically not
viewed as violence at all. Violence is customarily conceived
as an event or action that is immediate in time, explosive and
spectacular in space, and as erupting into instant sensational visibility.
We need, I believe, to engage a different kind of violence, a violence
that is neither spectacular nor instantaneous, but rather incremental and
accretive, its calamitous repercussions playing out across a range of temporal
scales. In so doing, we also need to engage the representational, narrative,
and strategic challenges posed by the relative invisibility of slow violence.
Climate change, the thawing cryosphere, toxic drift, biomagnification,
deforestation, the radioactive aftermaths of wars, acidifying oceans, and
a host of other slowly unfolding environmental catastrophes present
formidable representational obstacles that can hinder our efforts
to mobilize and act decisively. The long dyings – the staggered
and staggeringly discounted casualties, both human and
ecological that result from war's toxic aftermaths
or climate change – are underrepresented
in strategic planning as well as in
human memory.

—Rob Nixon
Slow Violence and the
Environmentalism of the Poor

Water Levels

<pre>
                                        the River
                                          might
                                          empty
                                      expend its
                                    sedimentary
                                          breath
                                      become a
                                           spine
                                        stripped
                                           open
lower yourself into the grasping mud   to an
     translate the heat that passes through your opening
                       fingers to a reddening sky
</pre>

                                                    open your
                                                     mouth
                                                      fill
                                                     with
                                                   the other
                                                    crevices
                                                   be swept
                                                     with
                                                  roe scraped
                                                     from
                                                   the River
                                                      bed
                                                    scoured
                                                     leaves
the River   will   overflow   and
                              drag   sediment
      break   the lines   of   its   management

              submerge   the   V-channel

```
                                                    fill your
                                                    pockets
                                                    with
                                                    pebbles
                                                    and
                                                    fingerlings
                                                    remove
                                                    your
                                                    shoes
          tie them up with the strings of a piano   fold away
dragged across the lake (1875)                       your
       box them up with the last crated whitefish (1910)   words
            tamp them down in a root wad (2017)  they   have no purchase
```

Caddis Fly

someone asked
me a question

answers glint off the trees in
the sun and i cannot
hold them

i cannot find it

they fall through
my bent fingers

i would like to write

beautiful things on tiny pebbles

and leave them in the River

i would like to be broken into
pebble-sized pieces

if i could be a substance of any use – to be the
pebbles on the back of a caddis fly

harbinger of healthy
water

How to Read the Gaagigewang River

1. close your eyes
   count nail heads like heartbeats
   visible divisible by desire

2. make assumptions about unity and ice jams
   report drunk boaters, bait your hook
   with smelt, do not snag submerged geographies

3. choose popular convention
   climb a small lighthouse, imitate dark
   read tourism pamphlets

4. cup your hands
   let history leak through the cracks
   mechanically separate mill wheel and boom truck

5. site the plumb line
   walk in situ (file artful under useless)
   follow the River's running, there is only here, here

6. bend your ear to the ground
   pat down the rumble of conquered geographies
   rumbling back

7. ask good questions (don't answer) blind yourself
   with the naked eye, landscape evidence is slippery
   is your grief (which is your love) a measurable attribute?

August 15

She resides in herself.

To read a River   read the banks
            sounds   sprayed into the air
    what she moves   over

    pen her words as   fluid
    blood   recirculating
            through the earth

August 21

bengwaa endso-shkwaa-gimiwang, dry after each rain

The strip of birchbark, wiigwaas, has been stripped off the collection of axioms tied to the cedar. The papers are no longer attached to the cedar but are resting in the crook of a branch. I suspect the ties have been undone by someone afraid to perch on the steep bank in front of the tree to remove the papers themselves. I photograph the changes to the paper and stitch them back with the remaining twine. The paper shows signs of wear and staining as well as bird droppings. It looks like something has been eating the paper. Despite these changes, I expect the paper will last a long time, as it is able to breathe and move and dry after each rain.

Shifting Baseline Syndrome

desire paths cut across
generational gaps
i walk the path he walked
but it's not the path he walked
without linking *A* to *B*
we continually rework the starting line
the falls are beautiful today

the raised arm, the shadow
like breath
i walk her path
and it is her path
B becomes *A*
the path shifts imperceptibly
the falls are beautiful today

the scale of experience
doesn't allow for extrapolation
statistical modelling flatlines
at yesterday. i dream
we all wake missing digits
without the ghost pain
the falls are beautiful today

we start our days knowing
no differently
identification requires
generational memory
we don't know the words
we have lost
the falls are beautiful today

species shift to generalities
leaf
ivy
fish
we don't know the worlds
we have lost
the falls are beautiful today

II.

our memories are
the projections of
what we expect
the falls but
not the River
the hook in
the mouth but
not the progeny
the thin underbrush
not the thinning
the melting snow
not the salt

progress requires collective
amnesia and master
classes in "now"
new myths are
created to make
coherent the incoherence
of climate change
decisions made with
one eye closed
the waters flatten
the incremental loss
what is common
is uncommon was
common it is
not natural but
socio-ecological extraction
economics are the
recurring baseline "ecosystems
do not rewind"

August 22

I can sometimes taste the differences in the lake water
a hint of fish rot in the fall, clay and sediment
        rushed up to shore during storms.

I think about my body, mostly water.

      Hydrologic cycles map taps, clouds,
rarely, the water-treatment stations, the runoff,
        not the intimacy of the exchange, the swallowing, the evacuation,
           the cellular uptake, the writing of our bodies through water,
      our writing onto water, the cycles of microplastic and hormones.

I am as much the lake and the River as anything else.

I understand myself as little as I understand water.

      Water moves in multiple directions, speaks in many languages,
           communicates in porosity, water is eco-logical.

I wonder what I'd find in my body if I drank directly from the River each day for a year.
Perhaps heavy metals, the salt runoff from the winter plowing that sends dirty salted
snow down the bank, the manure from cattle on the upper River, the septic runoff
from old camp systems along the lake.

Hydro Legible

trek mud and dog shit from the River to the car to the kitchen

evaporate

collect cedar at the River **the social life of water**

percolate colonial history through canal pipes

precipitate microbes, microplastic, rot

walk along the River and drag what I drag from home

squat and pee in the snow on deer droppings

draw treaties through waterlines

wipe myself with the snow and leave bright **fish mouth capital**

re/write the body in daily ablutions

vitamin b traces, gather branches fed by water the road salts

income flows elsewhere

the embankment breathe in   exhale   moisture   water

water writes

freezes   water moves   runs into the lake draw the water from

the taps from the lake filtered through fish and feces

colonial mathematics (conditions for precipitation) land + timber rights (1874) =

zebra mussels clay the microbiology of my urine my blood my

twelve settlers + lumber mill + grist mill × removal of Anishinaabeg

breath   pee   microplastics   hormones   fish   decay   microbes i drink the mill (2020)

microplastics water hydrologic cycle cycles through   trek mud

rites   rights

colonize water as resource and dog shit from the River to the car to the kitchen

hydrologic cycle Removal

collect cedar at the River make tea   walk along the River

un-name   **ourselves**   **generative**

and drag what i drag from home   squat and pee

water seeps through the triadic cycle

in the snow on deer droppings   wipe myself with the snow and leave

bright vitamin B traces, gather branches fed by water   the road salts

i drink deer into sedge

the embankment breathe in and   exhale

moisture   water freezes   water moves   runs into

the lake draw the water from the taps from the lake   filtered

through fish and feces   zebra mussels   clay   the

microbiology of my urine my blood

water communicates in porosity

it is eco-logical   **write water**

my breath   pee   microplastics   hormones   fish

hydro legible

decay   microbes   microplastics   water

September 6

She slows along the long curves and speeds up around the sharper bends, hushing along the grasses. On the upper River, she is quiet and calm, slow moving. The sound of the River is bird calls and wind, the movement of my paddle through the water. On the Lower, once she drops noisily from the limestone ridge, the River sounds along the shallows, changing from murmuring to rushing, hushing, burbling where the River changes from the limestone bottom to pebbles to clay. I drop into the River from the bank midway up the trail and float with her down to the bridge. In the deep curve where she carves up the clay, I hang onto branches and let her rush over me.

October 1, Conversation with Ed Burt

I visit ninety-two-year-old Ed Burt, descendant of Manitoulin settler farmers. A highly respected gardener and farmer with a history in antinuclear organizing, Ed is a storyteller with many memories of the River and how it's changed over time.

I remember
where the parking area
is now – I remember that being
a pile of hydro poles. That's where
Ontario Hydro piled their poles. They
had full length and short pieces too – the
deadheads. Wasn't even a path down to the
falls. I used to climb over the logs and slide down
the hill to the bottom of the falls on the way down
from working and sit there for a little while. Then
come back up.

I never was around that River very much because I
didn't live down there then. When I was young I spent
most of my time over around Nameless and Tobacco Lake
and a bit around Wolsey. That was my habitat when I was
growing up.

Somebody thought we should put some big boulders in
the fast-flowing water so it would inhibit the current and
make eddies behind the stones where fish could rest or
stop. They needed some big stones. Harold Noble had
a truck and I don't remember what tractor I had, but
I loaded up, I don't know how many loads. I took
the tractor down and I took them out in the water
and dropped them. I don't know if anybody took
them out or not. Don't know how far up we
went. We went up probably as far – if you
went to the Park Centre and went down
over the hill – we went up about that
far and put all these boulders in
the fast-flowing water.

Not
sure when we put those
stones in … in the 60s I think. The salmon
had been introduced. There has always been
some rainbows. Always been rainbows. Haven't always
been smelts – they're introduced too. But always been suckers.
Always been my view that that was the only wild fish that utilized
the River. They came up to spawn in the spring. Always water then.
Spawned by the hundreds and still do and lay their eggs and an awful lot
of the eggs are real sticky and stick to anything, stick to the stones on the
bottom, but the fast water moves a lot of the eggs so a lot don't stick and get
washed out and that's where they catch the rainbows in the spring. The rainbows
come to feed on that spawn and of course the rainbows could come up but I don't
think that they ever depend on it like brook trout depends for its entire habitat
winter and summer, but I don't think the rainbows do that. They move back into
the lake for the winter. I don't know whose bright ideas was that we put them
stones in the River. The suckers come in about five minutes after the smelts go
out. Up by the metal bridge – above that bridge – there's a flat area and you
can go down there at night and there be hundreds of them up in there.
People used to use pantyhose and a thimble – you push a piece of
pantyhose into the thimble and fill the depression with sucker
eggs then a piece of good strong thread and tie it and cut it
off so you have a bag of the roe and you put it on your
hook and go to mouth of the creek and you
can catch rainbow in the spring.

Not

salmon
always

water

spawn

night
push

cut it
off
mouth

October 3, Salmon Spawning on the Lower Kagawong

waakoonskewag maazhinmegosag, spawning salmon
maazhinmegos, coho salmon
gidaajwan, upstream

I move my hand along the page, following the salmon's efforts to move up a forty-foot section of the River over thirty-five minutes.

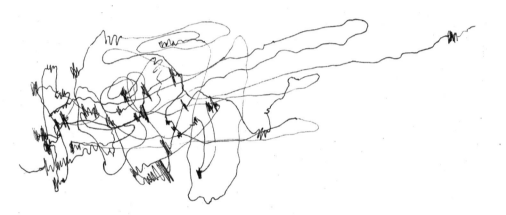

Spawning Salmon

tourists snap
photos
to the rhythm of   gaping   mouth

seagulls hopping   rock to   rock
we return to this
claimed territory

some compare   gasping   mouth
the sudden force   flipping   tail
to the plight of a minor god

but my flesh is   already   soft
my carcass   i will soon be
orange at the edges

my bones will
become a   curved   line
question on River rocks

i prefer the quiet twilight   dark   night
when all that is heard
is the River   splashing   tails

a seagull swallows my   rotting   River
eye
and laughs

Ed Burt, Salmon Stories

There
never was pickerel in Lake
Kagawong and they introduced pickerel.
In the 60s I think. They got pickerel from Spanish
River – they were River pickerel, but they've been putting
pickerel in the last ten years and they've been catching quite a
few in June in the last few years. I heard a story where they got a great
big pickerel at the south end. It weighed sixteen pound. It may have been
one of the earlier older ones or one of its early offspring. The pickerel now
are in the lake to stay. I know the Streams folks have done a lot of work and of
course we've introduced salmon to the Great Lakes and they come up there and
spawn but that's a new revelation. They didn't do that before they introduced the
big salmon. I've never thought that ... I guess it's a good idea. They would have been
better off ... If you're rich enough to own a thirty-thousand-dollar boat and troll for
hours and catch one – well, it's not my idea of fishing. They come up. There's a small
type of salmon. They're only about ten inches long; but then there's the big guys and
the cohos and the chinooks. They just come up and spawn and the young go back
to the lakes. But as far as the River goes I can remember once when the water
was really low and the River froze right to the bottom. If there'd have been any
brook trout they would have died. These salmon are just programmed to go
up a stream and most of the streams that salmon lay in have very little
food – not much of a food chain because the water is moving fast
in some cases. So what feeds the young fry is the dead bodies
of the parent fish. If they didn't die and provide food
for the fingerlings the salmon wouldn't survive
either. They pay a pretty
high price.

River   River

                              story

                                                        water
              River

                                              bodies

              high price

Abscise

cut away
the
space between
loss of
decline

abscise

the lengthening night

unmask
yellow

October 5

I keep returning to the alphabet with these installed poems, as shorthand for language, for conversation, as an invitation to collaborate. For the building of meaning, of worlds that can be created from twenty-six letters. These letters are also a fallback, code for what I can't speak. I have been confronting my lack of words; this inarticulation born of grief – environmental grief, coupled with my limited capacity to interpret and name the biotic world. The naming, ordering, and classification of the world through western ontologies has been justifiably critiqued. I'm not sure if I'm seeking to order or to understand. Perhaps I'm confronting the disarticulation, the falling apart of what I know, or think I know.

I have walked with naturalists who embrace the biotic world, love her through their delighted language. I have neither the species-specific intelligence, nor the knowledge of botany to communicate what I experience, intuit, and observe. My language is not of this land and doesn't speak in verbs. Perhaps my use of the alphabet collapses meaning rather than expands it, but I feel a different sort of intimacy, a gentle pleasure in these encounters. A chance to write verbs and process over nouns.

Just as the River shapes me and the process and the works, there is a continual unfolding between me and the poems, between me and the River. The work continues to unfold too. Letters erode, are pecked away, a strip of paper floats downstream to be read by fish in the bay. The revisions and edits, the writing and rewriting continue, and I witness only moments of it.

October 8

THE WIND IN CONVERSATION WITH A MAPLE

October 11

CONVERSATION WITH SAPSUCKER, MONTH THREE

baapaase, woodpecker

Fall Leaves

miizhmish niibiishan, white oak leaves
dgwaagi, be autumn

the oak fell in the storm
but not before the tent
caterpillars stripped
through the spring leaves
+ the unusually high
August + Sept winds ripped
them to shred.

October 15

I think about the long walks of the walking-book writers, their difficult treks, the conquering of self and geography. My walks along the River have always been deeply meaningful, even if the trail is short. Each time I walk the River I notice something. The scent shifting with the falling leaves, the rotting fish, the speed of the water. The light, the birds. In these returns, I am witness to the minute and shifting nuances of the River. Aware and sensitive to cues and changes.

The banks rise up from the River, steeply in some places. On the east side there is a series of hills that run perpendicular to the water, their valleys running towards the River, variously flowing with runoff or dry depending on the season. Nearer the mouth of the River the hill fills with ramps and ferns in the spring. Now it is filled with yellow and orange, brown with the beginning of decay.

Today I wander through the bush on the east side of the River, up and over deadfalls. My feet find their own way now, I've walked here so many times. I always end up in the same places, and along the same deer tracks. I run my fingers over the mosses and barks and listen to the birds and squirrels rustling in the leaves collecting below the poplars and ash, the maples and oaks. The River rustles too, below the bank.

Borer Tracing

Tree Bark, Nagek

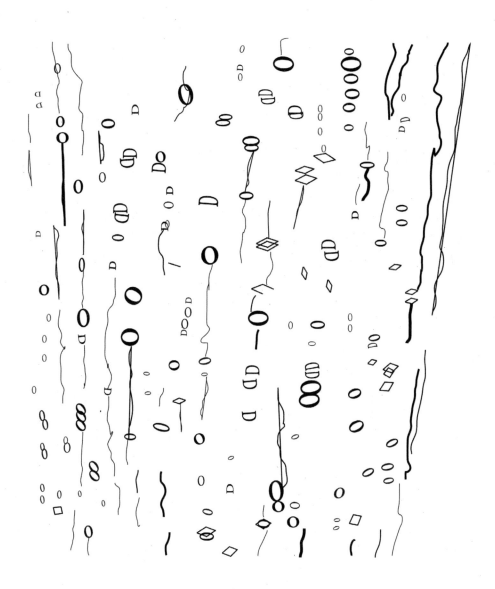

October 30

ndakwewaa, look for somebody's tracks

Things That Become Something Else

my life is a collection of small tributaries
a map, a palm without the hand
a series of leavings, streaming away

do the tributaries know their direction?

the River is quiet today
the salmon are decayed
even the seagulls have gone

the trees have little colour this year
tent caterpillars, drought, the constant
winds of September

they ask us to know them differently
to reference texture
knowledge through absence

my father walks ahead, as he did
when i was a child
moving more slowly

he wants to climb the ridge to the field
bow season directs us
to skirt the River instead

the trail disappears before the falls
we hear voices across the River
the dog fumes of fish rot

II.

at the bay, the streaming
water of the River meets the rushing
current of the lake

the waves become suspended
arcing between to and fro
neither River nor lake

the standing waves
ripple in place
an illusion of stasis

by late December, the collecting
ice has become a sheath
over the ridge of rocks

smoothed by the still-running
water in the shallow River
this is a new ice ridge

the rocks placed
to slow the water, to create pools
to create resting spots for salmon

which is the memory? the ice or the
running water?

the seagulls are gone, but
there are crows on the ridge
always in the shadow of my vision.

November 16

CONVERSATION WITH CASCADE FALLS, A FEEDER ON THE WEST
SIDE OF THE RIVER, MINUTE ONE

Waabgan ngii-maanjiwaa ziibiing, I gather clay from the River; and form a tablet
into which I carve the alphabet multiple times. The cascade completely soaks me
and the camera with the icy-cold water.

MINUTE THREE, HOUR EIGHTEEN

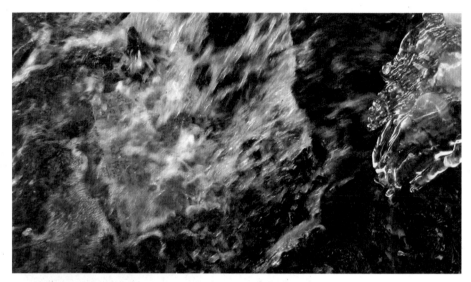

DAY FOUR

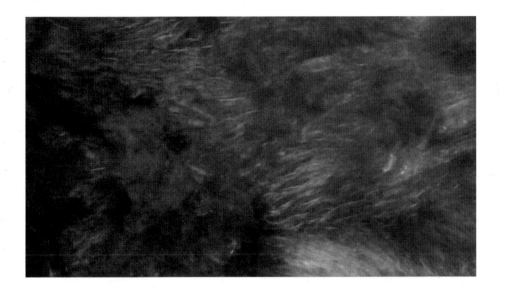

November 18

CONVERSATION WITH ED BURT — OH JESUS IT WAS PRETTY WILD

I remember being at
the one meeting when we were
talking about all the little places where
people went in to have picnics and were being
purchased and people were building cottages and
there was less access to the lakes. We were talking about
this and wondered if we could purchase some recreational
property because it's one thing to have a bunch of farms but
if there wasn't any place where you could go to the beach ... I was
driving to work and I thought holy smoke why don't we buy this Bridal
Veil Falls but Ontario Hydro had it. And it was just at the time that they
phased out the hydroelectric operation down in the stone building and
they had some diesel generators in there and they were using electrical — but
Ontario Hydro was getting into the nuclear business — this nuclear dream that
everybody had that this was going to be utopia for all mankind forever. I read the
stories they were going to have nuclear-powered suns in the northern hemisphere
and they were going to warm up sections of the north and be able to grow things
up close to the Arctic Circle. Oh Jesus it was pretty wild, so there was no real use
for that hydroelectric plant; it was closed. And they used that area by the falls to
store their poles. I went down to the conference in Toronto and got talking to some
of the government officials and they said it's agriculture redevelopment and you're
talking about buying recreational property and I said yes I am because man can't
live by bread alone he's gotta have some entertainment and joy and Manitoulin is
being taking over at the access areas to the lakes. We pick him up — this government
rep — then we drove down to Kagawong here and we — oh they were all dressed
up but we climbed over the poles and could see the falls — not very good, but we
got as close to the bluff as possible so he could see. And we got to the car and
we looked at a map I had — a rough sketch — down to the big flume that carried
the water to the hydroelectric at the stone building. A rough sketch of what
Ontario Hydro owned. We got in the car and one of the fellas said, how
much of the property do you expect to purchase? I said, I don't know.
Certainly, the falls and we can take the poles out and we can put in a
set of steps and people can enjoy the falls. The other fella said, why
don't you purchase it all? And I said yes, why don't we purchase
it all? So I made two more trips to Toronto after that. This is
something I don't tell very many people. I know the falls
the way it was and the paperwork Joe done, but
we ended up buying it. Part of it turned over
to the township. Maybe the township
owns it all.

holy smoke

utopia
stories   powered suns
north
Oh Jesus

yes

fellas

yes
all

all

November 20

I tuck a copy of Manitoulin Streams' River rehabilitation plan under a root wad installed in the River by Manitoulin Streams to create protection for small fish, a resting pool for salmon (themselves an introduced species like my cardboard letters, the root wads, and the vortex weir). I don't know why I'm attracted to doing these pieces in the cold water. But I get used to the cold and the cold water, and there is nobody along the River but me and the River. When I helped plant trees along the banks as part of the River's rehabilitation I learned terms like *root wad* and *vortex weir*. This large bark-stripped tree is almost bone-like. The cold runs up my fingers into my arms. The blue air is comforting. By spring the root wad has been moved downstream by the force of the freshet. The papers are gone too.

November 30

The early ice has melted, the water being warmer than the air; the River is still open and running fast, but for a short time ice crystals break off the trees, float, and follow the River downstream.

The paper and wooden letter poems are "unfinished." They too continue to write themselves, transform, move, relocate, disintegrate.

Are these still poems if they're only read by water molecules, sediment, the bobbing head of the solitary duck that stayed behind?

December 1

FORECASTS HAVE ENDED FOR THE SEASON

i translate water into a thin line of text

North Channel   it is silver

like the River at dusk

silver-and-blue breath

in print it is dark

where the water is light and transluscent

moving, where my words are still

as though rock does not have its own motion

the mechanics is recognition

the River here may be the River there

may not be all things being unequal

in valuation of resources, place, and time

December 2

The yellow-bellied sapsucker has gone south for the winter. It has long finished its work on the tree, likely even before I tied the paper to it, given its heavily bored bark. Perhaps it's the insects the woodpecker was after that have been working the paper.

By February someone has removed the insect poem.

December 13

Poems and letters continue to be removed by other walkers to keep the River trails "natural." I'm not bothered by the erasures and removals caused by strong winds, otters, rushing water. These human removals teach me more about human ways of thinking than about the ecosystem and its processes.

"The meanings conveyed by these words [*wilderness* and *wildness*] are human inventions which are rooted in a particular cultural context. In other words, there is no perception of wilderness that does not take its meaning from whatever we believe civilization to be ..."
—**Patricia Jasen**
    Wild Things: Nature Culture, and Tourism in Ontario, 1790–1914

There is no word for Nature in the Anishinaabemowin dictionary – there are words such as earth, zhashki; Mother Earth, Shkakmigkwe; land: ki.

I become increasingly circumspect (read: stealthy) about where I install poems. I find ways to bind poems to trees using vines and hide them under branches. I cover my tracks, hide when other walkers are present. I post fewer in-progress images on my social media pages. It's true the manufactured alphabets I leave at the River don't naturally occur at the River. This leaving of letters is an awkward thing, uncanny.

Other poems left behind:

Metal grates. Hydro-generating station. Paths.
Garbage cans. "Watch for Poison Ivy" signs.
Sliver of candy wrapper. Chinook salmon. Cigarette butts.
Root wads. Wing deflectors. Canal. Dam.

The porosity of human-natural boundaries and these constructed binaries between the so-called human and natural worlds, the movements between earthly bodies (including human bodies), lead me to how, not if. I continue to document the decomposition of these paper and wooden alphabets.

December 17

ALPHABET ON ICE, MINUTE THREE

Language is porous.

December 19

Increasingly my process on the River is about relationships. I am less observer, moving more into responsiveness. The longer I spend on the River, the more I energetically and physically feel the troubling separation of human|nature. At times I feel observed, noticed, felt. My response is increasingly shaped by what I see and learn with the River. I trace the porosity of my body and the aquatic one with which I am in relations as a writer, walker, and someone who lives downstream, drinks the water, and cycles her through my own household, through my body, and back into the water table, the air, and in turn the River. I begin to shift from noun to verb.

December 21

it is incremental, but at the last
darkness is longest

we gather past the cusp of darkness
but the cold hasn't come

shore ice converses tentatively
if there is a cycle now, it is freeze and thaw

i too converse tentatively

December 23

ICE CRYSTALS FORMING ON CEDAR BRANCHES

I've been watching ice crystallize on branches overhanging the River, becoming large bell-like formations, the branches swinging back and forth with the strong winter current. I type the alphabet hundreds of times onto a long strip of old cotton and ask Kyle Burt to help me hang the fabric from the tree. I've begun to experience a deepening of the symptoms which will change many things for me in the next few years. I'm concerned that I'll slip from the iced tree.

DAY FOUR

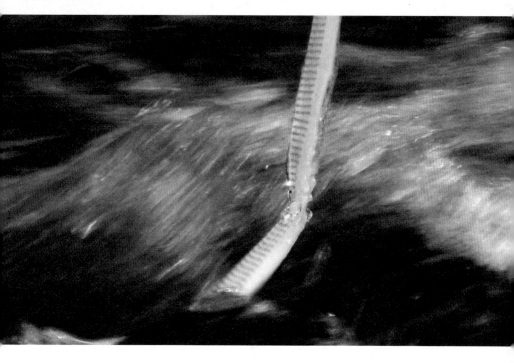

Crystallization

particle joins particle   growing language
    i cannot find a word for the ice that forms on branches hanging over water

  on the River language is motion   change a world of verbs
            not a story of stacked nouns claims

      meaning cystallizes   a responsive arrangement of
           particles inviting deposition

       conversing between formed   formless forming
           shifting multivocal not separate

       i am beginning to understand   what it means to lose the
      capacity to remember to fill language with the body

      the sense of being lost unable to translate ourselves
            into different forms

                ice   water
                vapour

January 20

zhibii'ganag, alphabet, letters

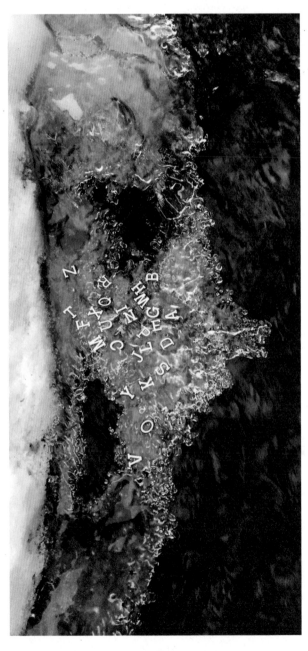

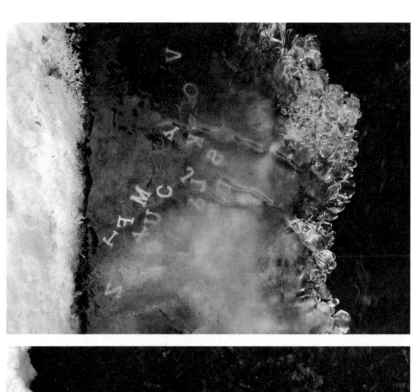

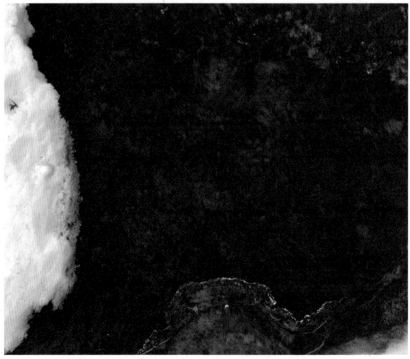

Balls of Ice Forming

Ice forms below the culvert that crosses under the walkway, fed by the steam coming from Cascade Falls, a small side-stream of water that feeds the River.

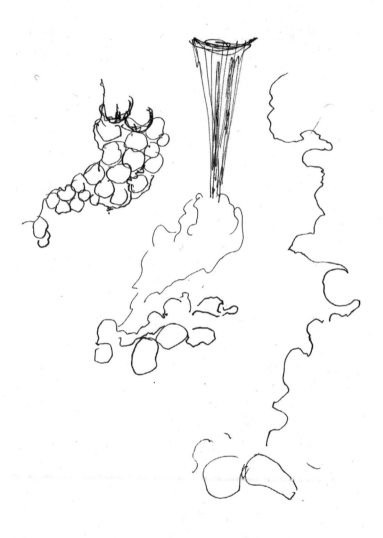

the ice below the pipe is freezing
into crystal balls.

February 5

mshkawaakzi, maazhnmegos, be a hardwood tree

As I enter the second year of this process with the River, I feel quieter. Not quite subdued, but more still. I revisit many of the places where I've installed poems, retrace my steps, follow otter paths. I lie in the snow beneath the trees and look up through the branches to the white sky and feel the River seeping into my bones. I'm not quite sure what I'm doing, but I'm okay not knowing. I don't know when this process will end, while knowing that an "end" is arbitrary. When I walk away, the River continues. She resides in herself.

February 16

INK ON ICE, REVISITED, MINUTE FOUR AND FIVE

February 17

February 22

OTTER TYPOGRAPHY

ngig, River otter

I enjoy following the otter runs all along the west side of the River, the quieter side, people-wise. I place small wooden letters at the entrance/exit of one of the burrow holes, and a piece of my hair as an introduction. I hope for some otter typography. I wonder, however, if this is a bit invasive? If the smell of my hands, my feet, my hair, and of course the letters will keep the otter away, away from this hole anyway.

I return the next day and surprise the otter coming up the bank. I return twice more. A couple of letters (*N* and *V*) have moved. This movement could have been from the wind, not the otter, as there are almost no tracks. I decide to stay away for a few days to see if the otter will return to the hole. I return and replace the letters along the path after the recent snowfall.

MARCH I, MARCH 8

New otter (and deer) tracks. New letters. A week later they are heavily tracked by otters and deer, some letters have moved.

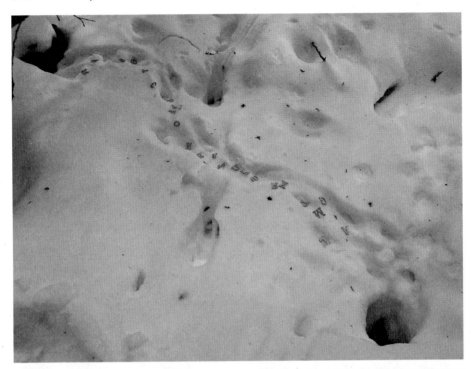

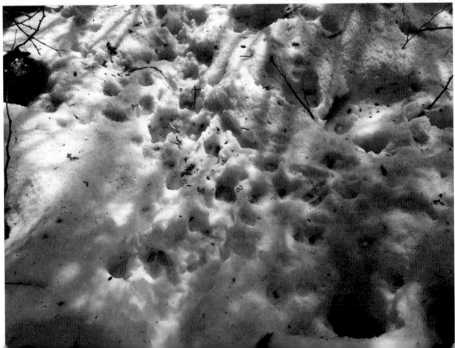

March 30

FROM MY HAMMOCK ON THE EAST SIDE OF THE RIVER

soft on soft
cedar breathing like morning
nuthatch bounces teardrop

yellow eats white
granular motion

you do not feel watched
trails on the River are iced confidence
one must not emerge the same
bark releases itself into moss

i see the world carving away
hope for bedrock where there is sediment

the River abandons kisses of cedar boughs
cones of rotted snow stand
along tracks of coded relief
you are soft under my curving veined hand
the River is finished with me

March 31

The trail has been closed by the Township in response to the pandemic.

Perhaps I knew this was coming, perhaps the River knew too. Perhaps it is this sense of change that gave way to the feeling of her being done with me.

The River is herself, always herself whether I'm there or not. Most days I feel listened to, heard, observed when I'm at the River. Although I spent time in my hammock hung between two cedars above the River, feeling the damp, smelling the trees, I felt cold, apart. I am struggling, wondering if these poems, these scattered letters have any meaning.

I wonder if this "project" is complete, if it's ending.

March 31

The River returns to herself.

i reach
language
dogwood
red. a
in the dry
by yellow
doubled.
River is
from an

back into
reach like the
from green into
sparrow rustles
rushes. bordered
tape i am
prayer to the
an intercession
interloper.

M'Chigeeng First Nation Band Council Resolution #4501

On April
7, 2021, the Chief and
Council passed Band Council resolution
No. 4501 supporting the M'Chigeeng First Nation
and its members' treaty rights to fish for sustenance
during the provincial state of emergency and stay-at-home order.
What this means is that Chief and Council assert on behalf of the
First Nation and their members their treaty rights to fish and have the
sovereign authority to do so. This treaty right is firstly an inherent right of our
people. Secondly, the right is protected by Section 35 of the Constitution and by
Section 25 of the Charter of Rights and Freedoms. The Emergency Management
and Civil Protection Act cannot deviate from the Charter as described in section
7.0.2 (1) of the Act. M'Chigeeng First Nation has historically accessed the rivers,
lakes, and streams in our treaty Territory to exercise our treaty right to fish since
time immemorial in various locations in our Territory. We will continue to support
our band member harvesters with this inherent right and will require them to do
so by wearing a mask, social distancing, and not gathering in large groups while
exercising their protected right. This also means that the Council expects that
our members will be respectful to anyone they may be in contact with while
peacefully exercising their right. These requirements must be met by our
members. We have not been consulted, nor advised of any order that
any townships and/or municipalities may or may not have invoked
in relation to the Emergency Management and Civil Protection
Act in our Treaty Territory. Our Council has provided
a statement to the Ontario Provincial Police
(OPP) in relation to any attempted
charges.

March 27

CONVERSATION WITH OTTER AND DEER TRACKS, CONTINUED

By April 5 the final letters have been removed, perhaps by another "illegal" walker skirting around the yellow caution tape. I avoid the paths and walk up the steep ravine at the edge of the park, then back towards the River.

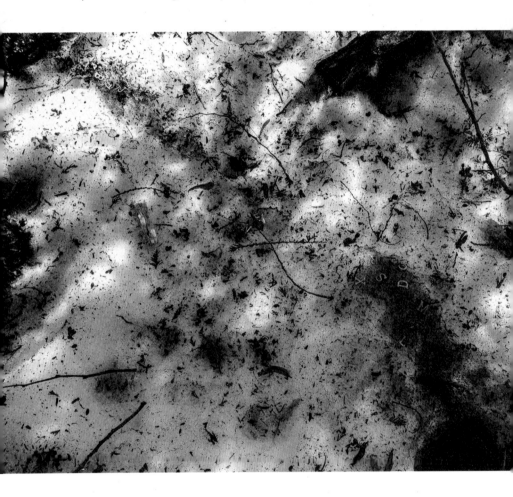

March 28

Over a number of months I begin to relinquish directing the focus of the camera. I float it down the River, hang it from trees. The River documents herself from the bridge.

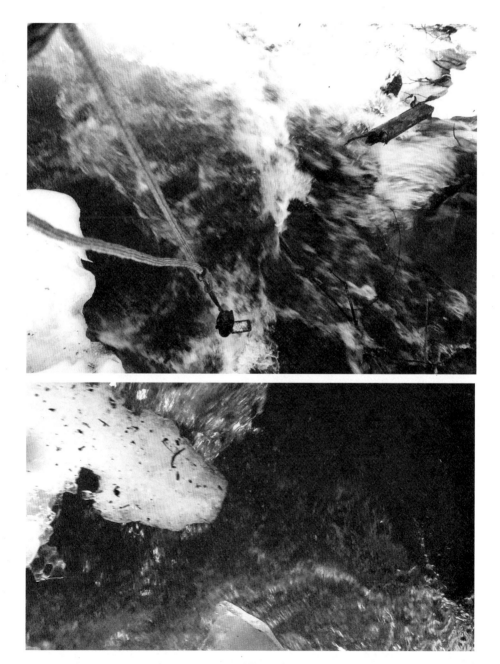

April 5

SOUNDING WITH SUBSOIL

naamkamik, under the ground

spruce roots twist
stones suspended, nuclei of soil
there is a sense in the early spring of active
waiting. i see things from the corners of my eyes
i want to film things that aren't moving

this is like waiting for a lover. the earth
remoulding, decomposing leaves becoming
something else. everything becoming
something else. seeds cued by warming soil
the breeze a warm humusy breath

under the earth, things unseen
dreams, circulating blood

prepare

Soil

shignaawshag, earthworms

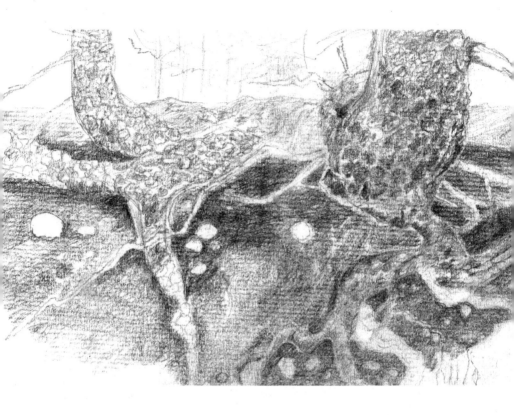

May 20

nigiikowaa, I discovered tracks of somebody

Although the trail is still closed due to the pandemic, I cut through the bush again. I have a clear view across the River to the west trail and can hear a long distance since the trees haven't fully leafed out yet. I find it hard to be so little on the River now, with the park closure.

Conversation with Ed Burt

HOG PEANUT

About
halfway along the River
it changes. It comes down along pretty
rapidly and when it gets to where it levels off
there's some sort of alluvium deposits. There are plants
that come from all over the lake, the seeds float down the
River and they go over the falls and they whip down that fast
section and they get to where that sort of alluvium deposits are, the
soil and debris has stopped and that's where there's quite a few different
plants and flowers growing. The River there is quite an ecosystem there and
I don't know much about my plants, but there's several plants that grow along
there and maybe they've been there for a long, long time but the one plant
that's there, hog peanut, I don't know how rare that plant is, but in my view it's a
special plant. I like to go look at it. It's a legume, it's a vine with two sets of fruit
and two sets of flowers and they're different. I think the peas that're in that
pod may even be poisonous and there's another flower that comes out right at
the ground. Unless you part the grass you can't see it, and it produces a little
underground tuber and that's where it gets its name. It's a peanut and
people used to say that if there were ever any pigs around they'd dig
it all up for those little peanuts. It'd be pretty difficult to come up
with a plant that is a Manitoulin symbol but that hog peanut
is a beautiful thing. It's the only plant I know that has
two kinds of pods and two kinds of flowers … and
that's one of the most beautiful plants
I know.

float

don't know

long time

don't know

Unless

name

only

know

Hog peanut plant

Conversation with Ed Burt

BEAVER STORIES

Down
where it levels out
there has always been a population of
beaver. It's shallow so there's not a lot of food
or roots for food so the beaver, they swim way out in
the bay and go out both sides of the bay and bring shoots and
things back up the River. There's a small population of beaver. It'll
always be small because beaver have to keep working and eating to
keep their teeth wore off. They're constantly chewing ... it isn't the kind of
a stream that is a good place for beaver. They need a place where there's a
lot of new-growth poplar and willows. They eliminate their food source, and
one stays and maintains the dam but the colony breaks up and they scatter and
move upstream or downstream and make a new dam. It could be five years, it
could be ten and maybe after fifty. The spring runoff washes the dam out but the
trees are all growing again and there's a new population of willows and poplars
so they build another dam. So it's a kind of a boom-and-bust economy. They're a
great Canadian symbol – they're kind of mindless workers but they do have a
tremendous work ethic and they don't pay any attention to their population.
They don't assess the area for the necessities that it can provide. So they
overpopulate and they keep on a collision course until they can't go
any further and the whole damn thing breaks up. And maybe
one or two of the colony finds a place to repopulate. Never
learned a damn thing. Do the same thing again. Yes,
they're a good symbol 'cause there's a hell of
a lot of Canadians that think the
same way.

shallow

roots

eliminate   source
colony

washes

mindless

collision

Rethinking the Beaver

mik, beaver
aanjtoong aansokaanan or dbaajmowinan, changing a story

"Biologists classify beavers as a
Keystone species. Beaver ponds create
wetlands which are among the most biologically
productive ecosystems in the world. They increase plant,
bird and wildlife variety, improve water quality, and raise
salmon and trout populations."

"'Beaver have an overwhelming influence on wetland creation and
maintenance and can mitigate the effects of drought.' Citing climate
change models that predict increasingly frequent and persistent
droughts, they recommended that we make more of an effort to
coexist with beavers – by installing perforated pipes to regulate
flow, for example, instead of removing problem dams – and even
recruit them to help with wetland rehabilitation projects.
While the language may be academic, the message is
clear: we need to rethink our relationship with
beavers and learn to appreciate them as
stewards of our most precious
resource."

June 2

mskwaadesiinyiik, painted turtles
jiime, to paddle

I begin to paddle the upper Kagawong. There are no COVID access restrictions for the boat launch so I can drop my kayak into the water from the dock. The dock provides one of the only ways to access the upper River, as most of the land along the banks of the upper is privately owned and the municipality can be reluctant to establish and maintain public access to waterways. It is rare to see anyone along this stretch of the River between the falls and Lake Kagawong, even during the height of summer, even though Lake Kagawong is a large lake and popular for fishing. In all the times I've paddled here over the years, I have only seen the occasional boat and sometimes people tenting at the campsites close to the lake. Most of the properties along the banks are well treed, the houses are closer to the road than to the River. There are farms and cows. There are many swampy inlets along both sides. The River is fairly shallow – only six or seven feet deep in spots – but still deeper than the lower River. The shadows of fish and turtles cross the loose sediment-filled bottom.

There are so many birds flitting across the water, in and out of the reeds. I know very few birds, but I recognize the red-winged blackbirds, the blue heron, the crows, the kingfishers, and the prehistoric-looking sandhill cranes that pass overhead, their calls echoing along the water. Painted turtles with their yellow-streaked heads sun on the half-submerged logs, a snapper swims below the kayak. I begin to record bird calls and play more with video. I document the poems floating down River, wondering if time-based media might help me explore process more readily. But after a few months I find that I prefer leaving poems that may or may not be seen. Poems that undergo a process outside of human time. I also don't like being pulled away from the River to sit on the computer with an editing program for hours on end.

Rosgen Classification System

it appears still on the upper River   the surface rippled

by wind wings and motor   slow and solid in winter   the

current moves imperceptibly until you float with her

pulled along towards the dam   the falls

coralled in the slow upper   there will be lilies

in summer   rushes

a snapper eighteen inches wide   fingerlings darting

like synchronous thought in and out of the reeds

the bed is not the bottom but loose decay two feet down

there will be spring birds in the woods and marshes

along the banks   herons and red-winged blackbirds

marsh wrens   and the Wilson's snipe that leads you

forward   flush in the spring by late summer

leaving sediment in the shallows   mud   where the banks

curve on the lower faster course the River catches up to

herself speeding up on the inside curve   frothing

oxygen over rocks   rippling signals   catches her breath

with the resting fish behind stones   tags overhanging

cedars   whispers to frogs on the banks

Abstract: "... alluvial streams are open systems that adjust to altered inputs of energy and materials, and that a form-based system largely ignores this critical component. Problems with the use of the classification are encountered with identifying bankfull dimensions, particularly in incising channels and with the mixing of bed and bank sediment into a single population. Its use for engineering design and restoration may be flawed by ignoring some processes governed by force and resistance, and the imbalance between sediment supply and transporting power in unstable systems ... The Rosgen classification is probably best applied as a communication tool to describe channel form but, in combination with "natural channel design" techniques, are not diagnostic of how to mitigate channel instability or predict equilibrium morphologies."

the swelling spring is frothy and silver riding up the

banks   rushing remnants of snow   submerges grasses

making islands of the lows   gathers soil where the bank

is bare   rearranges the Riverbed

there is no classification more concrete than poetry

than the sound of the River   my hand under the surface

the green breath of basswood

Call and Response

the call and response of the Kagawong and the

Spanish, Blue Jay Creek, M'Chigeeng stream   arteries

"According to the local press, the Ontario Ministry of

feeding the liquid mind of the lake returning to each

Natural Resources and Forestry said the fish dying

other through mouth and body breathing the

was a result of 'environmental stress associated with the

sediment of history

rapid warming of surface waters, following a late

bottomed out   the limestone breathing filtering

ice out and cool spring ... the data available suggests that

the history of the Huron   industrial St. Mary's and

there are existing water quality issues with the lake.'

Spanish sediment contamination

Billings Township Mayor Ian Anderson

dioxins and furans stormwater runoff filters the

said, 'there was work done on Lake Kagawong two

stories of the cranium shield   old stories erased from

years ago and the whitefish population is very good. I

limestone   but history is molecular my body is

am definitely not convinced there is a problem with

stirred by the sound

water quality. There is no evidence' ... The Ministry

of a small engine at dusk   i can almost smell the fish

then went on to talk of high phosphorus levels leading

the reflection of water droplets on a taught line

to low oxygen and other sources of phosphorous are

cannot reconcile diesel and desire like the tourist

septic systems, exposed soils, agricultural runoff, and

blind to the River above the falls as though

atmospheric deposition.'

history and future aren't small circles

June 5

CONVERSATION WITH A MARSHY CHANNEL ON THE UPPER RIVER, MINUTE ONE

I type the alphabet dozens of times onto a long strip of thin paper and paddle to one of the marshy inlets.

DAY ONE, MINUTE FOUR

DAY TWO, HOUR TWENTY-THREE

LILY PAD, NO TRANSLATION REQUIRED

June 6

JUNE 8, DAY TWO, JUNE 13, SLIPPAGE

By August I am unable to access this swampy channel off the upper River as the water level has gone down about a foot.

June 10

bmikwaansan, small tracks
nimkwaadensaan, I make small tracks
niibin, be summer

Another trespass onto the River. No signs of further removals by humans.

The River feels different after several months of the trail being closed. I imagine the playful otters and the flitful birds and the quiet fish gathering and nattering freely. The early summer plants and flowers are pushing up through the spruce needles and decomposed leaves. The River is quiet here, a hushering.

Each time I return, my tracks are harder to find, but my breath sounds louder. Only the faintest trace of my repeated walking on the track over the winter remains. It is possible to be gentle with our tracks.

My shadow registers. My shadow tracks as desire.

June 13

O IS A VERB, MINUTE ONE

mshiikenh, snapping turtle

I place small wooden letters on lily pads floating on the upper River, documented somewhat perilously from a half-submerged deadwood, not far from where I spot a very large snapper. As still as the River seems here, the letters float off the pads within seconds and begin to flow downstream. This placement on pads becomes movement, flow.

June 19

SECOND CONVERSATION WITH LILY PADS

nbiish-waawaasgone, lily pad
nbiish-waawaasgoneyin, lily pads

I place a second set of alphabets on the pads so I can track the movement of the letters.

MINUTES FORTY-SIX AND FORTY-SEVEN AND ONWARD

The letters travel slowly and steadily downstream.

June 19

I witness so little of these poems. I am beginning to understand more
deeply that the alphabet is not just a stand-in for what I don't know, but an
invitation to meet the biotic world within a third space that is neither me
and my English, nor the biotic world and its biotic languages. A middle place
of translation, relation, and unknowing. This unknowing is becoming more
comfortable and meaningful.

Much of my time on the upper River is spent floating. I can't easily get out
of the kayak, as the shoreline is swampy. I have pulled in and napped under
a massive maple tree shading the River, but otherwise I float. I listen to the
birds. I watch the clouds pass by me through the water. I paddle into the inlets,
ducking under dogwoods and willows, manoeuvering between the rushes and
sedges. Painted turtles plop from their log-sunning into the green water.

June 21

CANALIZE, MOSS AND YOGURT

Biological interaction: Mutualism is a type of biological interaction in which two or more partners of different species benefit each other.

I paint the stones with a mix of moss and yogurt. There are trees down across the canal, so I can't paddle all the way along this canal constructed to divert water from the River to feed the hydro-generating station. The water from the canal runs under the building where I used to work, then under the road to the bank of the River. There is a spot in front of the building where the motion of the water below makes the gravel seem to breathe.

June 29, Attachment Dynamics

MOSS AND YOGURT, PARTIALLY SUBMERGED LOG ON THE UPPER RIVER

I like the expansiveness of the upper River. The lower is narrower, more shallow. The water never stops flowing down towards the bay. On the upper sometimes the wind plays with the surface so that it can feel like the water is moving back towards the lake, or that it's not moving at all, but as soon as I stop paddling the current moves me downstream. The water feels thicker here.

There is a constant conversation between the sky and the lake, with the birds and clouds stitching the two together.

June 7

CONVERSATION WITH CATTAILS

pakweyshkook, cattails
Pakweyshkoong, place of the cattails

Cardboard letters woven into cattails on the upper River, spelling "translation." I think more and more about the third space between the River's language and mine.

July 7, 2021

The letters are de-compos-*ing*

August 15, 2023

When I return two years later, this stand of cattails is gone entirely.

August 19

I've started floating my camera on the water, in an attempt to see from a different perspective. The River documents my paddle and a bee, aamoo.

September 8

I increasingly feel the River watching me. Sometimes I feel she knows when I'm here. Sometimes I feel we listen together. I greet her each time I come. I run my hands in the water, wipe the water over my face and neck. I pull a strand of my hair and send it down the River. When the birds hear me, they are quiet until I am quiet, then they return to their foraging and twittering and flitting tree to tree. I continue to walk slowly along the edge of the River, on the east side, where it is bordered by small bushes, poplars, and cedars, grasses trampled in spots by deer. Squarish limestone boulders are scattered throughout the shallow River. I walk across their slippery surfaces to the other side.

I don't know if it's my imagination but there's a kind of hum, a colour I can hear when I'm near the River. A mossy green colours the breath moving in and out of my lungs.

I have been tying my camera and the video recorder to branches. The camera gently spins and records. I float and follow the camera down the River. I take it underwater. I submerge myself. I record this exchange.

September 28, Poetry Exchange

n'kwewaa, meet a snake on a body of water
masdamoonh, northern water snake

Between takes, I sit shivering in the water.
A water snake shoots away from the heat of my lap.
We surprise each other.

Perspective

THE RIVER LOOKS BACK AT ME

THE RIVER LOOKS UP AT ME

October 3, Tracks

bigashknisin, decompose

After nine months, the letters are beginning to deteriorate and de-compose.
I can no longer lift the kayak onto my car.

October, One Year Later

The River continues to change, her course slightly shifting each year, new growth, new deadfalls across the path. The Township is building a new walking bridge across the River. The new trail built to meet the bridge cuts through the quiet low area between the ridge and the water, and through the otters' playground. This quiet low-lying area of the ravine between the ridge and the River, between the trees and the bay is no longer as quiet. I feel disoriented.

October, Two Years Later

I return
to the River as I've done
most weeks for years, this time to slowly
walk to and through all the places where I'd left
alphabets.
The longest lasting had been the tracked letters and those
woven into the cattails. The woven letters were protected from the
elements, able to dry after each rain, and were hard to see, camouflaged
as they were, wefted into the warp of the rushes. But that entire stand was
gone when I paddled the Upper over the summer.
The tracked letters lasted longer because I'd walked over them repeatedly,
embedding them into the snow and ice, and then into the grass, but these are gone
now too, decomposed, removed.
There is no formal ending to this process along the River, only what I arbitrarily chose
as a starting point and an ending. The residue of poems might still be circulating in
the River, in the clouds, pieces of decomposing letters forming part of the decaying
leaf litter below the trees. The echoes might still be echoing. And I am still
listening, still learning, still opening to the lines of the River, her sounds.
I still do not speak River, or otter, yet my body hears differently now.
The listening body opens to language.
All the letters are gone now, decomposed, removed, or circulating. I
can find no other traces of the poems,
the letters, my tracks.
This is as it should be.
All that is left are the spaces where
language finds itself.

                    return
              River
                      time

        lasting

  elements

  embedding

                                              circulating
              decomposing   forming   decaying
                echoes
  listening   opening   sounds

        listening
                                        circulating
                    traces

        language finds itself

Ecological Foundations

1.   flowing under the words
breaking the palimpsest of landscape
is an ecology of River that flows beyond

2.   the pink and blue of maps
and knows no borders
under the weight of construction

3.   and below the frost line
worms and roots, granular deposits
limestone shelf with a breath of millennia

4.   stones rise
a morphology of slowly moving permanence
our readings are limited

5.   by our own capacity for breadth
the slow violences
come home on the earth

6.   oikos: house
knowledge: writing
geo: land

7.   what poetics are we writing?

The River is in the Language, the Language is in the River

vii = verb inanimate intransitive
vai = verb animate intransitive
vti = verb transitive inanimate
vta = verb transitive animate
ni = noun, inanimate
na = noun, animate

aamoo, na: bee, pl: aamook
aanjtoong aansokaanan or dbaajmowinan: changing a story
aatebgaa, vii: leaves fade, turn dull

bboon, vii: be winter; gbe-bboon, all winter
bengkamgaa gaa-shkwaa-gimiwan: dry after the rain
benijwan, vii: flow along
bigashknisin: decompose
biijmaagzens, na: smelt, pl: biijmaagzensak
biimskojwan, vii: be a whirlpool, flow in a circular pattern
bkejwan, vii: branch, fork
bkijjiwan, vii: flow over something
bkwebiigmi, vii: be dirty water
bmaaboozo, vai: float along, float by, float
bmaadnaa, vii: be a ridge of hills going along
bmijwan, vii: flow
bmikwaan, ni: footprints, tracks, pl: bmikwaanan
bmikwaansan, ni: small tracks
bmikwe, vai: leave footprints, leave tracks
bneshiinh, na: bird, pl: bneswak
bwaayaak, na: white ash

daankosdooñ wiya wda-aansokaan, vai: add onto another's story
dbasshkaa, vii: be low grass
ddibew, ni: shore, riverbank, near the water's edge
ddibewe, vai: go along the shore
dgwaagi, vii: be autumn
dkwiindmaa, vii: be shallow water
dpashkaa, vii: be damp grass
dpijwan, vii: flow through an opening

ekwishin, vai: an imprint of one be left somewhere, leave an imprint somewhere, there be an imprint of someone's body somewhere
esbaanh, na: raccoon, pl: esbaanyik

gaachdeyaagmaa, vii: be straits
Gaagigewang Ziibi: Kagawong River
gaamaajwan, av: on the other side (of a body of water)
gaawaandgwaatik, na: white spruce
gaming, ni: lakeshore
gidaajwan, av: upstream
giigdowin, ni: convesation, pl: giigdownan
giigoonh, na: fish
giigoonke, vai: fish
giigoonwi, vai: be a fish, turn into a fish
giizhkaandag, na: eastern white cedar, northern white cedar
gmiwan, vii: rain, precipitate
gzhiijwan, vii: flow fast, run fast
gziibiiydiza, vai: erase one's name from a list, erase one's name from a record

jidmoonh, na: squirrel, pl: jidmoonyik
jiigaajwan, av: by a stream or river, near a stream or river
jiigbiik, av: on the shore
jiime, vai: to paddle

ki, ni: land, ground, earth, one's sovereign land
kinonaan waawaashkeshwan: s/he is speaking to the deer
kinoonaan ziibin: s/he is speaking to the river

maajiijwan, vti: flow away, start to flow
maajjiwan, vii: start to flow
maazhnmegos, na: coho salmon
maskdamoonh, na: water snake
mdwejwan, vii: make a sound in flowing
miizhmish niibiishan, na: white oak leaves
mik, na: beaver, pl: mikwak
mkomiins, na: icicle
mkomiiwaaboo, ni: ice water
mkomiiwan, vii: be ice covered, be icy
mkomiiwi, vai: be ice, turn to ice, be ice-covered, be icy
mnajwan, vii: flow nicely, flow well

mngagmaa, vii: grow, be large (body of water)
Mnidoo Mnising: Manitoulin Island, spirit place
mnookmi, vii: be spring, be springtime
mooshk'an, vai: there is a flood, it is flooded
mooshkago: spring runoff
mshiikenh, na: snapping turtle, pl: mshiikenyik
mshkawaakzi, vai: be a hardwood tree
mskwaadesiinh, na: painted turtle, mud turtle, pl: mskwaadesiinyiik

n'kwetgweyaa, vii: the rivers meet
n'kwewaa, vta: meet a snake on a body of water
naamaazhbik, av: under the rocks
nbiikaa, vii: be a watery place; be lots of puddles
nbiish-waawaasgone, ni: species of water lily (probably yellow pond lily, Nuphar variegatum), pl: nbiish-waawaasgoneyin
nbiish, ni: water, an amount of water
ngig, na: otter, pl: ngigok/ngigwak
nigiikowaa: I discovered tracks of somebody
nigkogmaan vii: be a certain size (body of water)
niibin, vii: be summer
niisaajwan, av: downriver, downstream
nimkwaadensaan: I make small tracks
njijwan, vii: flow from a certain place
nmegos, na: brown trout, trout
nmegshens, na: rainbow trout
nwiiyaw, nid: my body

pakweyashk, na: cattail, pl: pakweyshkook
Pakweyshkoong: place of the cattails
pichi, na: robin

shignaawshag, na: earthworms
Shkakmigkwe, na: Mother Earth
shpashkaa, vii: be high grass
sin, ni: rock, stone
swejwan, vii: (river) fan out

tigweyaa: the course of a river

Waabgan ngii-maanjiwaa ziibiing: I gather clay from the river
waabgan, ni: clay
waakoonskewag maazhinmegosag: spawning salmon
waannijwan, vii: (river) bend
wan / wanaabte, vii: be foggy, be misty
wanbiisaa, vii: be a drizzling mist
wiigwaas, ni: birchbark
wiikwebiiyaa / wiikweyaa, vii: be a bay
wiikwet, ni: bay
wiinjiishkwaak, vii: be mud

zaaday, na: poplar
zaaghigan, ni: lake
zhashki, ni: dirt, earth, soil
zhibii'gan: alphabet letters, pl: zhibii'ganag
zhiiaaajwan, vii: flow through
zhiishiibak, na: ducks
zhijwan, vii: flow in a certain direction, flow a certain way
zhitgweyaa, vii: running in a certain direction
zhkashkwaa, vii: be damp grass
ziibaajwan, vii: flow through
ziibi, ni: river
ziibiikaan, ni: ditch
ziibins, ni: brook, creek, stream
zoogpo, vii: the event of snowing

Pronunciation

Short		Long	
a	as in rush	aa	as in all
i	as in sit	ii	as in week
o	as in book	oo	as in row
		e	as in red

Glossary of River Nouns

the webs expressed in land
the capillary membranes
the conveyance loss
the porous spaces
the use of water
the tension
the sediment
the sustained flow
the capacity of water
the appropriative doctrine

fragments of other rocks transported
from their sources and deposited in water

Glossary of River Verbs

fish
to fish
to flow through
to flow in a certain way
to flow through an opening
to make a sound in flowing
to be a River running in a certain direction
to flow in a circular pattern
to turn into a fish
to flow nicely
to fan out

to erase one's name from a record

Ed Burt

Hope
I helped you.
There might not
be any truth to it.
It's just a story.

Daankosdoon wiya wda-aansokaan, to add on to another's story

Sources

Note: URLs have been included when possible.

Mnidoo Mnising, Manitoulin Island, Gaagigewang Kagawong: From *Soil Survey of Manitoulin Island: Report No. 26 of the Ontario Soil Survey*, Canada Department of Agriculture, Ottawa, 1959, Library and Archives Canada/Soil Map of Manitoulin Island, Ontarion/OCLC 1007348156.

Kinoonaan Ziibin, Conversations with the River: Anishinaabemowin words and phrases used here and through the book were translated or shared with me by Alan Ojiig Corbiere, Clarice Pangowish, and Clarice's father Clarence C. Pangowish, a first speaker. Josh Eshkawkogan, also a first speaker, provided the phrase "Ndoo-nsastann ziibi" and translations for "resilience" in response to our conversation about this book. In addition to the words shared directly, Alan directed me to these references: *Nishnaabemwin: Odawa and Eastern Ojibwe Online Dictionary*, dictionary.nishnaabemwin .atlas-ling.ca; J. Randolph Valentine, *Nishnaabemwin Reference Grammar* (Toronto: University of Toronto Press, 2001); and Mary Ann Corbiere, *Introductory Nishnaabemwin* (Sudbury, ON: University of Sudbury, 2001). Clarice and Clarence reviewed all of the Anishinaabemowin in the book: unless different in quotes and references, spelling and grammar was chosen based on local usage of M'Chigeeng, the closest community to the River. Ojibwe and Odawa are spoken on Manitoulin; there are dialect variances between communities and a range of spellings for these words.

Conversations with My Toes …: Cindi Katz, "Playing the Field: Questions of Fieldwork in Geography," *The Professional Geographer* 46, no. 1 (1994): 67–72; Harriet Hawkins, "Geography and Art. An Expanding Field: Site, the Body and Practice," *Progress in Human Geography* 37, no. 1 (2013): 52–71; David N. Livingstone, *The Geographical Tradition: Episodes in the History of a Contested Enterprise* (Oxford: Blackwell, 1992); Felix Driver, *Geography Militant: Cultures of Exploration and Empire* (Oxford: Blackwell, 2001). Various facts and terms are drawn from the following sources: "The Hydrologic Cycle," *PhysicalGeography.net*, accessed May 7, 2009, www.physicalgeography .net/fundamentals/8b.html; "How Long Does It Take for Water to Be Evaporated Then to Be Put Back on Earth as Precipitation?," UCSB ScienceLine, accessed April 18, 2005, scienceline.ucsb.edu/getkey.php?key=894#:~:text=According%20to%20these%20web%20sites%2C%20the%20average%20 time,atmosphere%2C%20and%20then%20leave%20it%20again%20as%20 rain; and "Simulated Historical Climate and Weather Data for Kagawong," *MeteoBlue*, accessed April 11, 2024, www.meteoblue.com/en/weather /historyclimate/climatemodelled/kagawong_canada_5988608.

For more on reading landscapes, see John R. Stilgoe, "How to Read the Land: A Lexicon of Landscape as a Word, Concept, and Path to Discoveries," *The MIT Press Reader*, December 30, 2019, thereader.mitpress.mit.edu/reading-landscape/.

First Treaty: This petroglyph sculpture was carved by Anishinaabe artist Michael Belmore as part of a permanent installation on the Gaagigewang Ziibi, Kagawong River installed through a River rehabilitation project by Manitoulin Streams in 2015, and part of a larger sculpture trail project I curated and led as the Artistic/Executive Director at 4elements Living Arts on Manitoulin Island; 4elements and its community partners received the 2017 Ontario Lieutenant Governor's Ontario Heritage Award for Excellence in Conservation for the project. The carving is a reproduction of the turtle petroglyph at Kinoomaage-waabkong (the Teaching Rocks), Peterborough Petroglyphs National Historic Site of Canada. Text and translation used with permission of the Township of Billings, Alan Corbiere, and the translation team. Image used with permission of the artist.

Prophesy: Robin Wall Kimmerer, excerpt from "Shkitagen: People of the Seventh Fire" from *Braiding Sweetgrass: Indigenous Wisdom, Scientific Knowledge, and the Teachings of Plants*. Copyright ©2013 by Robin Wall Kimmerer. Reprinted with the permission of The Permissions Company, LLC on behalf of Milkweed Editions, milkweed.org.

Instructions for the Poet Wanting to Sound with the Gaagigewang Ziibi: Thank you to geographer and poet Eric Magrane who influenced this series of poems with his "Various Instructions for the Practice of Poetic Field Research," *1508*, April 13, 2012, poetry.arizona.edu/blog/various-instructions-practice-poetic-field-research.

Directive, 1861: Original source SPPC, 1863, No. 63 (Bartlett and Lindsey, October 12, 1861), Library and Archives Canada, documented in Shelley J. Pearen, *Four Voices: The Great Manitoulin Island Treaty of 1862* (Ottawa: S.J. Pearen, 2012), 9.

Treaty Clauses Four and Five, 1862: Transcription of the 1862 Articles of Agreement and Convention for the Surrender of the Great Manitoulin Island and the Islands Adjacent [LAC, RG10, 1846, T9939], documented in Pearen, 166–167.

Manitoulin Island shewing [sic] *portion ceded, 1862*: © Government of Canada. Reproduced with the permission of Library and Archives Canada (2023). Source: Library and Archives Canada/Robert Bell fonds/e011201296.

Auguste Kohler, 1862: Archives of Ontario, F968, MS159, Can. 1 – XV 35 (Kohler to Becks, November 20, 1862), transcribed in Pearen, 118.

Petition to the Government, June 1866: Documented in Pearen, 118. Original source LAC, RG 10, 333, C9582 (Ojibwe petition and English translation), 78–105.

Manitoulin Superintendent J.C. Phipps, November 15, 1873, Manitowaning, to Deputy Superintendent of Indian Affairs William Spragge Regarding Magawong (Kagawong): Research by Shelley Pearen. Original source Library and Archives Canada, RG10 vol 1906 file 2302.

William Spragge to J.C. Phipps, November 27, 1873: Research by Shelley Pearen, shared with the author. Original source Library and Archives Canada, RG10 vol 1906 file 2302.

Surveys and Plans: "Indian" Trail and Burying Ground, 1879: MANITOWANING - APPLICATION OF ROBERT HENRY TO PURCHASE LOTS 27, CON. 16, BILLINGS TOWNSHIP, ALSO LOTS 5 AND 6 CON. 8, AND 2, 3, 4, CON. 9, CAMPBELL TOWNSHIP © Government of Canada. Reproduced with the permission of Library and Archives Canada (2023). Source: Library and Archives Canada/ Department of Indian Affairs and Northern Development fonds/e002532140.

Plan of the North Part of the Township of Billings, 1916: F. Bolger, D.P.S. © Government of Canada. Reproduced with the permission of Library and Archives Canada (2023). Source: Library and Archives Canada/Department of Indian Affairs and Northern Development fonds/e011205603.

May 29, 1872: William Plummer to Joseph Howe, RG10, Vol 1864, file 336, research by Shelley Pearen, email communication with the author.

Simon J. Dawson, Member of Parliament for Manitoulin and the District of Algoma, Speaking of the 1862 Manitoulin Island Treaty in Parliament, 1886: Official Report of the Debates of the House of Commons of the Dominion of Canada, March 8, 1886 (Ottawa: MacLean, 1886), 64, cited in Pearen.

Remains of Henry Brothers' mill in Kagawong, at Bridal Veil Falls, 1900–1910: Image from the George Irwin fonds, uploaded to the Commons as part of the Archives of Ontario's GLAM Wikimedia Commons project, accessed November 22, 2023, commons.wikimedia.org/wiki/File:Remains_of_a_ mill_(I0014063).jpg.

How to Produce the Kagawong River: Written in response to Don Mitchell, "New Axioms for Reading the Landscape: Paying Attention to Political Economy and Social Justice," in *Political Economies of Landscape Change: Places of Integrative Power*, eds. James L. Wescoat Jr. and Douglas M. Johnston (Dordrecht, The Netherlands: Springer, 2008), 29–50, which is an important response to Peirce Lewis's "Axioms for Reading the Landscape: Some Guides to the American Scene."

Gaagigewang Historical Plaques: In my role as the Artistic/Executive Director at 4elements Living Arts, I designed, led, and curated the Billings Connections Trail project, securing funding from Canada 150 and Ontario 150. The source of funding was problematic and the project a challenging one. One aspect of the partnership with the Township of Billings, the local Recreation Committee, and the Old Mill Heritage Centre included the installation of historical plaques. Approval of the plaque text, including Indigenous content (the latter based on research by Shelley Pearen and Alan Corbiere), by a dedicated committee of community representatives was a difficult, yet meaningful, process of discussion, frustration, tears, negotiation, and eventually learning, compromise, and consensus. Pushback by the Township, which sent the text for legal review, sparked protest by the committee and community members from Kagawong and M'Chigeeng First Nation (to read more, see Ruth Farquhar, "Column: Billings Council's Actions Disgusting and Shameful," *Sudbury Star*, July 9, 2017, www.thesudburystar.com/2017/07/10/column -billings-councils-actions-disgusting-and-shameful). Eventually the Indigenous content was given the go-ahead, and the plaques were installed with the larger series of The Old Mill Heritage Centre's historical plaques, along with a series of sculptures that invited artists to explore the intersections of land, environment, and Truth and Reconciliation. As part of a year-long community engagement process, Alan was invited to share the Treaty history of Manitoulin Island. Over eighty (primarily settler) people sat through a rainstorm under a mostly dry tent, riveted by his three-hour talk. Alan, Shelley Pearen, and I approached the Billings Town Council in 2022, requesting that the Indigenous plaques and their translations be made available publicly to support language learning, which the council agreed to. Although Alan and his team translated all thirty-five (primarily settler) plaques into Anishinaabemowin, only the plaques that include Anishinaabeg history are included here, with permission from all parties involved.

March 4: John Berger, *Ways of Seeing* (London: Penguin, 1972), 7.

How to Tell a Geospatial Story: Written with and in response to Jonathan D. Phillips, "Place Formation and Axioms for Reading the Natural Landscape," *Progress in Physical Geography: Earth and Environment* 42, no. 6 (2018): 697–720.

Gathered Words from Visitors to the Falls: "Rivers and Climate Change," *American Rivers* (website), www.americanrivers.org/threats-solutions/ climate-change/.

"By slow violence …": Rob Nixon, *Slow Violence and the Environmentalism of the Poor* (Cambridge, Mass: Harvard University Press, 2011), 2. © 2011 by the President and Fellows of Harvard College. Used by permission. All rights reserved.

How to Read the Gaagigewang River: Written with and in response to Peirce Lewis, "Axioms for Reading the Landscape: Some Guides to the American Scene," *Journal of Architectural Education* 30, no. 1 (1976): 6–9.

Shifting Baseline Syndrome: Masashi Soga and Kevin J. Gaston, "Shifting Baseline Syndrome: Causes, Consequences, and Implications," *Frontiers in Ecology and the Environment* 16, no. 4 (2018): 222–230. Daniel Pauly, "Anecdotes and the Shifting Baseline Syndrome of Fisheries," *Trends in Ecology and Evolution* 10, no. 10 (1995): 430.

October 1, Conversation with Ed Burt (and subsequent poems using Ed Burt's words): Interview with the author, used with permission.

November 20: Manitoulin Streams Improvement Association, "Kagawong River Restoration Sites," (Interactive GIS map), accessed April 11, 2024, streams .maps.arcgis.com/apps/MapJournal/index.html?appid=4a1fbfcdc2d041b-1b23a30ce4696f89d.

December 13: Patricia Jasen, *Wild Things: Nature, Culture, and Tourism in Ontario, 1790–1914* (Toronto: University of Toronto Press, 1995). Franklin Ginn and David Demeritt, "Nature: A Contested Concept," in *Key Concepts in Geography*, Second Edition, eds. Nicholas J. Clifford, Sarah L. Holloway, Stephen P. Rice, and Gill Valentine (Los Angeles: Sage, 2009), 300–311, us.sagepub.com/en-us/nam/node/50615/.

M'Chigeeng First Nation Band Council Resolution #4501: Excerpt from Tom Sasvari, "Billings Acknowledges First Nation Smelt Fishing Rights," *Manitoulin Expositor*, April 16, 2021. Used with permission. www.manitoulin.com/ billings-acknowledges-first-nations-smelt-fishing-rights/.

Rethinking the Beaver: Frances Backhouse, "Rethinking the Beaver," *Canadian Geographic,* November 30, 2013, canadiangeographic.ca/articles/rethinking -the-beaver/; Mike Callahan and Heidi Perryman, "What Good are Beavers?," The Beaver Institute (blog), accessed April 15, 2024, www.beaverinstitute .org/what-good-are-beavers/.

Rosgen Classification System: Andrew Simon, Martin Doyle, Mathias Kondolf, F.D. Shields Jr, Bruce Rhoads, and Munsell McPhillps, "Critical Evaluation of How the Rosgen Classification and Associated 'Natural Channel Design' Methods Fail to Integrate and Quantify Fluvial Processes and Channel Responses," *Journal of the American Water Resources Association* 43, no. 5 (2007): 1117–1131.

Call and Response: Excerpt from Ruth Farquhar, "Islanders Must Act to Protect Their Lakes," *Sudbury Star*, September 26, 2019, www.thesudburystar.com /news/local-news/farquhar-islanders-must-act-to-protect-their-lakes.

Conversation with a marshy channel on the upper River: I found out after making this piece that Marlene Creates documented a sheet of blank paper she'd placed amongst lilies about thirty years ago. She enjoys our call and response.

The River is in the Language, the Language is in the River: Anishinaabemowin is a complex language in which a limitless variations of words and meanings are made up by stringing together component parts – roots, medials, and finals, words often having a meaning that is larger, or more specific, than the sum of their parts. Words often need to be understood within the context of the sentence of which they are a part. The pronunciation guide comes from Mary Ann Corbiere, *Introductory Nishnaabewmin* (Sudbury, ON: University of Sudbury, 2001).

Acknowledgments

This book took an ecosystem to write.

First and foremost, my unending gratitude to the Gaagigewang Zibii and for the privilege of living here on Mnidoo Mnising.

G'chi miigwech Dr. Alan Ojiig Corbiere and Shelley Pearen for your painstaking historical research and for sharing it with the community and me.

G'chi miigwech to Al Corbiere, Josh Eshkawkogan (a first speaker), Clarice Pangowish, and her father Clarence Pangowish (a first speaker) for the Anishinaabemowin, with double thanks to Clarice and Clarence for the review of the spelling, grammar, and phrases. To Al, Clarice, and the crew of translators on the trail plaque project. To the Township of Billings which agreed to make the plaque text available for public use and language learning. To the plaque committee that worked so hard and came to consensus.

Thank you! Talonbooks, Kevin Williams, Catriona Strang, and Leslie Smith for supporting me as I entered the publishing river. Thank you to the Talonbooks poetry advisory board for recommending the book and taking a chance on me. Unending gratitude to Jordan Abel for the incredibly kind and generous offer to propose my book to Talon.

Deep gratitude to the very fine editing of Daniel Lockhart, Turtle Clan member of Eelünaapéewi Lahkéewiit (Lenape), a registered member of the Moravian of the Thames First Nation, and currently residing at the south shore of Waawiiyaatanong (Windsor, ON–Detroit, MI). His attentive and insightful response to my work helped reshape this book in meaningful and important ways.

Thank you to the members of my 2019 and 2020 Poetry CSA (Community Shared Art) Project, who responded to the early stages of this project with enthusiasm, kindness, and thoughtfulness.

Thank you to a full alphabet of friends who buoyed me through this project in so many different ways: A.F., Andy Smith, Anong Beam. Chris Turnbull, generous reader, connector, and champion. Ed Burt, Heather Thoma, Judy Bowyer. Jack Illingworth for shipments of poetry, plants, and sound advice on all things writing. joni m palmer, John Turner, Julia Winder, Karen Dominick, Kate Thompson, Mike Abel, Sarah Gabrielle Baron, Sharon Speir, Sheila Gruner, Shirley Cheechoo. Pam Jackson and Gary Furhman, for always believing in me. My Wiky koko friends Lisa Shawana, Lori Toulouse, Theresa Trudeau. For everything videopoem, Jackie Atkins, Jonny Zagula, Eric Reder, and Annette Maangaard. Marlene Creates and Don McKay for laughter and creative encouragement. Kendra Edwards, former über intern, who came to my rescue with InDesign. The dear neighbours who've adopted me and do any number of kindnesses that help me have time to write: Phil and Susan Smythe!, Bob and Denise Carriere, Kris and Norm Leclair. Neda Debassige, super pharmacist, who tries so hard to keep me healthy. A gang of friends and colleagues who pooled cash together in the winter of 2020 when I had a small house fire.

The Canada Council for the Arts and The Ontario Arts Council provided several grants during the process of writing this book and creating a series of video poems. The Writer's Trust of Canada came through at a critical juncture.

And Residencies! Sage Hill (virtual) summer 2021 was a joy – two amazing weeks of conversations about writing, hybrid forms, and the work of writing in the world, led by Jordan Abel. The 2021 Banff (virtual) Winter Writer's Residency with Waubgeshig Rice and Emma Healey was an ice floe in a long winter. Thanks to two physical residencies that provided much-needed time away from home to sink into this project: Halls Island Artist Residency and the Al and Eurithe Purdy A-frame Residency.

Thank you to the small presses and literary magazines that published earlier versions of some of these poems: The Blasted Tree produced a beautiful hand-bound chapbook titled "crystal + clay" with an accompanying video poem. Gap Riot Press printed a series of "floating" postcards called "River Writes" and hosted a conversation between me and the talented Anna Veprinska.

A number of the poems originally appeared, sometimes under different titles, in the following publications: *Arc Poetry Magazine*, *Terra North/Nord*, *The Capilano Review*, *Pi Review*, *Empty Mirror*, *talking about strawberries all of the time*, and *Hamilton Arts and Letters*. An essay about my process with the River was published as "Earth Writing | Writing Earth: Instructions for the Geopoet Wanting to Interview a River," in *Doing Performative Social Science: Creativity in Doing Research and Researching Communities*, 197–209, ed. Kip Jones (Oxford: Routledge, 2021).

Gratitude to my mom Dany, who nurtured me and my love of books and words, and my father, who brought me on my first walks in the bush. For my brother Elliott, who shares my love of the first River we lived on.

And finally, but not lastly, to my daughter Emilie – my love for you is an eternal River.

sophie anne edwards (she/her/settler) lives on Mnidoo Mnising, Manitoulin Island, in Northeastern Ontario with her dog Bea and a roster of other WWOOFers who help in the garden. Her first loves were books and the water until the birth of her daughter Emilie Aude. Her writing has been generously supported by the Canada Council for the Arts and the Ontario Arts Council and published by numerous journals and micropresses across Canada. Sophie holds an MA in Interdisciplinary Studies and a Certificate in Creative Writing from Humber College and is a Ph.D. candidate in geography at Queen's University.